These Things Really Do Happen To Me

Also by Khaya Dlanga

To Quote Myself: A Memoir (2015)

Shortlisted for the 2015 *Sunday Times* Alan Paton Non-Fiction
Award

'It's in Khaya's nature to be a storyteller; *To Quote Myself* shows
just how much he has nurtured his craft over the years. This book
is like my favourite thing: crisp white linen. Yes, the bed is freshly
made but the fun is getting into it and finding your own space. I
found my space so many times in this book. It's a must read!'
– ANELE MDODA

In My Arrogant Opinion (2012)
Part of THE YOUNGSTERS series

'This is just one in a series of entertaining pocket books, aptly
called *The Youngsters*. The youth-aimed series features prominent
young South African personalities and tackles issues that range
from the cultural and political, right down to hair weaves and
clubbing etiquette.' – *Business Day Wanted*

These Things Really Do Happen To Me

Khaya Dlanga

MACMILLAN

First published in 2018
by Pan Macmillan South Africa
Private Bag X19
Northlands
Johannesburg
2116

www.panmacmillan.co.za

ISBN 978-1-77010-631-4
e-ISBN 978-1-77010-632-1

© 2018 Khaya Dlanga

Editing by Kelly Norwood-Young
Proofreading by Sean Fraser
Design and typesetting by Triple M Design, Johannesburg
Cover concept by Donovan Goliath
Cover by publicide
Cover photograph by Saki Zamxaka

I am dedicating this book to the many stories my mother has lived. And to my co-stars – the people who have shared in my stories and have helped to make this project a reality.

Contents

Introduction

I think that life is ultimately a collection of stories we either create or find ourselves in. Some moments are funnier than others. Some moments have little joy, though we learn lessons. Sometimes there is nothing to learn; they're simply fleeting moments that we may remember for their uniqueness.

I have had the idea of writing a book with the title *These Things Really Do Happen To Me* for a while now. I remember telling some friends about how I had lost my mother's suitcase after being homeless. I'd left the suitcase in a church so that they could look after it, promising them that I would collect it at a later stage. I didn't tell them at the time that I didn't have a place to stay.

After a few months of sleeping in a flat that was being renovated, and on desks at the college I was studying at in Cape Town, I eventually managed to find lodgings with the help of some church members. But when I went back to the church to fetch the suitcase, it had mysteriously vanished. No one knew what had happened to it. I assumed it had vanished through the Bermuda Triangle of Christian generosity.

And then, a while later, I managed to find it again by coincidence when I was helping a family whose home had been devastated by a tornado. That story can be found in my book, *To Quote Myself*.

I often tell stories like this and people comment on the fact that I have so many stories to share. I say that I don't have better stories or more stories than them; the difference is just that I talk about and share my stories.

Part of the reason I felt encouraged to write this book is the comments that my long-ass captions on Instagram get. People often ask for them to be longer; they want more stories.

Instagram's Best Nine feature shows, at the end of every year, users' nine most popular posts from that year. Most people's best posts are of them, by themselves. But not me. In 2015, for example, only one Best Nine post featured my face, and I was not even alone. If I am not mistaken, my Best Nine in 2016 was like this for me too. There were only two pictures that featured my face – and, again, I was not by myself in a single one of the Best Nine. My most popular posts each year were captions about an event or a story I was sharing.

I get the picture. Those who follow me on social media find the people I am with attractive, and I happen to be in the way. Obviously, I don't have a face for Instagram. I am still going to therapy.

One of the primary reasons I wrote this book is because I feel that we have been through a lot of serious years and seen a lot of serious books published. My book is meant to be light-hearted, talking about everyday life.

There are some serious topics I touch on as well because I think they are important, even if I have to include them in a book that is largely meant to be light. Life happens whether we are being serious or having a good time.

We are each stars in our own lives, and simultaneously, co-stars in the lives of other people we encounter. Romances, tragedies, horrors and laugh-out-loud comedies are all part of our stories. My life is the same as everyone else's.

Life is made up of those funny or coincidental moments that find their way into our stories while we are on our way to do the shopping, the moments that stand out in what seems mundane. These moments deviate from our normal routines, disrupt the everyday, and make for memorable experiences. I am celebrating those moments in my life with this book.

Johannesburg
July 2018

.

The shining Vaseline Blue Seal kid

There are many stories my mother, Nonceba Dlanga, loves to tell about me as a little boy. One of these is about my cousins from the big city and me.

When I was about three or four years old, I was living in Dutyini near Mount Ayliff with my mother, sister and grandparents, Alfred Kaiser Boyce and Vuyelwa Victoria Boyce. My mother had decided to move in with her parents when her husband, my father, left for Johannesburg with another woman and stopped supporting us. My mother's sister, Nolulama Mshumi, was supporting her from Mdantsane, just outside of East London.

My aunt and her husband would drive down to Dutyini to visit my grandparents and sometimes they brought their children, who are my cousins. Obviously. There was Nobulali, Unathi and Mazwimahle, who is a month older than me. (Qiqa and Malubekho had not yet been born.) I would always hang around Mazwi because we were the same age.

I often played outside in the dust but when I heard my family from the big township were coming, my mother says I would go fill a small portable basin with water, wash myself, and then not so much moisturise as completely smear myself with Vaseline Blue

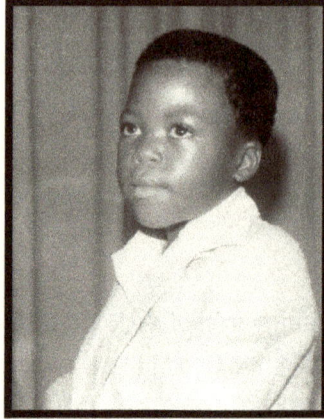

Glistening with Vaseline to impress my city-slicker family

Seal. I would then put on the newest clothes I had. I tried to look as presentable as possible.

My cousins looked really clean and beautiful from not having to live in the harsh conditions of village life. I thought that if I looked clean, and shiny from the Vaseline, they would take me back with them to the big city, where I would have a better life. I'd have hot, running water from a tap, electricity, and would eat meat often. I hoped they would not notice that I was not supposed to be part of them.

But, they always left without me and I realised that there is a certain layer of village that can't be washed off with a single bath.

Years later, I would become a big city-slicker myself. My mother says it was if I knew, even as a child, that I wanted to change my circumstances: 'Ndambona lo mntwana ukuba akasokuze aziqhathe.' ('I saw that this child won't cheat himself out of a good life, even then.')

My birthday is always weird

My birthday has always been weird for me. The reason only occurred to me recently.

When I was young, I lived with my grandparents in the village. My father lived in Johannesburg and had been absent from our lives for some time. My mother had moved to work in East London, which is roughly five hours away by car.

The year I turned six, my mother decided to throw me a big birthday celebration. It's something she had seen parents in the city do for their kids. My sister Sikelelwa's birthday was four months later but my mother didn't want her to feel left out, so we had a combined party. If you look at the photo on the next page (don't mind my aunt peeking at the neighbours through the curtain), you can tell this was a big deal because there is even guava juice on the table. And don't let me get started about the chips in the enamel dish.

It was on this day that a telegram was sent to the village. It was on this day that the grown-ups at my birthday were all called into a room. It was on this day that I heard a collective gasp from the grown-ups. It was on this day that I heard my mother's uncontrollable, pained cry from that room, while we were playing outside. It

My cousin, Unathi Mshumi, lighting the candles on my birthday cake

was on this day that we found out that my father had been stabbed to death. On my birthday. He was only 26, making my mother a very young widow.

A few years ago, I was making a Snapchat video about how awkward I get about my birthday. In the middle of making the video, I had a sudden realisation. I had always known that we found out about his death on that day, but I never made the conscious connection between his death and my feelings about my birthday until that moment.

That realisation, I think, is freeing me up to understand and let go of the discomfort I have about my birthday.

My father, the absent

My father, Zandisile Dlanga, disappeared in Johannesburg, and abandoned his wife and children. Tragically, he was murdered and would never have the opportunity to come back into our lives.

His father, Thambile Paulos Dlanga, died after being captured and tortured by apartheid police. He also died young – 44. Maybe the reason I try to do as many things as I do, is that a part of me feels that I, like my father and grandfather, could also die young.

I have three pictures of my father – none of them with us together. Perhaps he thought he still had time. I have a single memory of him: he was standing outside my grandmother's house and talking to my mother, next to my aunt's car. I remember being in my mother's arms when she passed me over to my dad, and then he held me against his chest. That's the memory.

The older I get, the more I hold on to this sole memory. In my memoir, *To Quote Myself*, I wrote about how unattached I am to it. Things change.

My mother says my father was kind, enjoyed reading, and was very loving and romantic (I must get that from him).

I do believe that our fathers, more often than not, love us more than they can tell or show us. Sometimes they may be overwhelmed

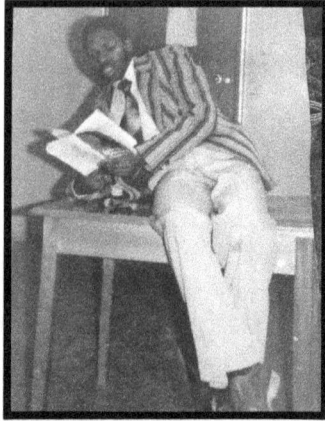

One of the few pictures I have of my father, Zandisile Dlanga

by the responsibility of fatherhood, and avoid it or flee from it. I think that sometimes they vanish completely because they are ashamed that they didn't or couldn't take care of us. Seeing the children they have let down probably compounds an unimaginable guilt in them.

Fathers can inspire much bitterness in their children when they don't become who they are supposed to be to us. But I do think it is important to love our fathers, regardless of their failings. Sometimes, simply by welcoming and loving them, we can encourage them to become better fathers. And that, in turn, releases us from the burden and poison that is bitterness.

Cars in the village

When my Uncle Senzangakhona and Aunt Nolulama, my mother's sister, visited us in Dutyini, they would do me the honour of allowing me to stay and play in the car. My mother tells me that I was about three years old, and I would show no interest in my relatives when they arrived because all my attention would be directed towards the vehicle. Once I was inside, it was difficult to get me to get out. I'd turn the steering wheel, touch all sorts of buttons and pretend I was driving. I'd do this until it was time for my uncle and aunt to leave for Mdantsane, which was a six-hour drive away.

My mother remembers that I would turn to her as soon as they left and say, 'Thula, anti, nam ndizokukhwelisa, nam ndizoyithenga mhla ndaya eGoli.' ('It's okay, aunt, don't cry, one day I will let you get in my car. I will buy one when I go to Johannesburg.') Of course, I was the heartbroken one; she was completely unbothered.

When I was small, I thought I was going to go to Johannesburg to work in the mines because most young men in the village did so.

Later, when I did grow up and start working, I worked in Cape Town for four years before moving to Johannesburg. It was only after I had moved and started working in Johannesburg that I got a car. I may not have ended up doing underground mining but I did

Standing in front of my uncle's car when I was three or four years old

go to Johannesburg and I bought a car – just like I'd said I would when I was three.

Growing up in Dutyini, we didn't see cars often. The only car we saw every day, a Toyota Hilux, belonged to Mr Chanca, the shopkeeper. The Chanca family was the most prosperous family in the village.

Mr Chanca's bakkie would deliver big loads of groceries to various homes. If you had ordered a big load – 25 kilograms of mealie-meal, 12.5 kilograms of sugar, a bag of cabbage and so on – he would deliver the load to your family home. The roads were bad so a 4x4 was the best and most practical car to have in the village.

The village dogs would always chase after Mr Chanca's Toyota, and we little boys would do the same. We would shout and ask the car – yes, the car, not the driver – to bring us sweets. Whenever we saw an aeroplane flying above us, we would also run after it until it vanished, and shout, 'Uze usiphathele amasweet nama chips, ne gwava jus!' ('Bring us sweets, chips and guava juice!')

If we wanted to see more cars, we would have to make our way towards the N2 or the road leading to Ntabankulu. Back then, this road was not tarred and cars, driving at speed, would leave plumes of dust in their wake.

We used to stand or sit by the side of the road, looking after cattle or sheep, making sure that they did not cross the road and get run over by cars. We would count cars or try figure out, from a distance, what makes and models they were. The person who guessed correctly first got a point. Naturally, I would always win this game. Even in these circumstances, I was more privileged than many of the other village kids my age because I got to go to Mdantsane and East London during the holidays – which meant I was exposed to different cars.

Sometimes the cars would stop and the people would take pictures of us. One day, after a photo of me had been taken – wearing oversized, somewhat torn and dirty clothes, with no shoes, and posing with clean, white children – I suddenly realised something was wrong with this picture. I must have been about seven or eight.

The people who did this were always white. The nice cars, with boats trailing behind them, with fishing rods sticking out the windows, with happy children, were always driven by – yes, you guessed it – white people. From that day on, I refused to have pictures of me taken. Even when I was offered sweets.

There were no white people in the villages. They were never poor. The only poor people were black. It didn't make sense to me because I didn't see what was so different between us. I simply could not understand. When I began asking questions, I found out about a thing called apartheid.

Snitching on my mom to get out of trouble

When my sister and I lived with our grandparents in Dutyini, my mother visited about once a month – to check up on us and to see if her parents needed anything from her. She worked in a pharmacy in Mdantsane, about 400 kilometres away from us.

Before she arrived, the homestead would be busy with people running around to ensure that my sister, Siki, and I were fine, and clean. If she found us dirty, she would be furious. No one wanted to face my mother's wrath. We would be washed, and an orange or cabbage sack would be used to exfoliate our skin, to remove the grime from dusty village life.

Once, before one of her visits, my sister and I were confined to the kitchen, after being washed clean and subjected to Vaseline Blue Seal petroleum jelly. We were glistening. Siki and I were told to stay put so that we didn't make ourselves dirty again by the time our mother arrived.

To distract us, we were given the tricycles my mother had brought for us on a previous visit. We were still extremely bored.

The joy of seeing my mother arriving home was short-lived because she was so mad to see that we were cycling in the house. To her, it seemed that her parents were being soft on us, allowing

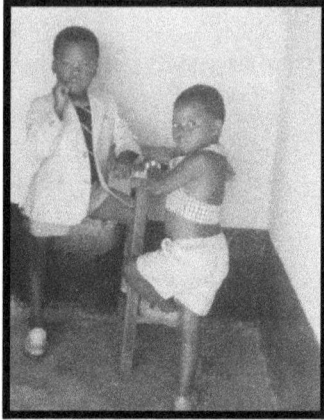

Siki and I, dressed up for one of Mom's visits

us to do what we wanted.

She started shouting, saying our gran was handling us with kid gloves. 'Phumani! Phumani okanye ndiphindela eMdantsane! Aga!' ('Get out or I will go back to Mdantsane! Aga!')

We began crying and hid behind the door while she was going off at us for being ill-disciplined. As if this was not upsetting enough, she realised that one of us had killed a recently hatched chick while we were cycling in the kitchen. (My gran had lots of chickens.)

She got even madder. 'Aga man! Nicinezele nentshontsho! Aga man!' ('Aga, man! You've trampled on a chick!')

It was at this point that I found a gap to get my sister and I out of trouble.

'Ndizakukuxela kumakhulu ukuba uyathuka uthi "aga"!' ('I will tell Gran that you just swore at us and said, "aga"!')

When my grandmother walked in, I told on my mom: 'Makhulu,

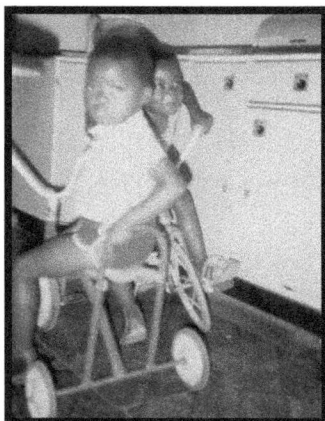
Being surprised by Mom while riding tricycles in the kitchen

uanti uthukile uthe "aga"!' (Grandma, aunt just swore and said, "aga".')

My gran, a very religious and kind woman, immediately started shouting at my mom for swearing in front us. 'What are you teaching these children if you swear at them and in front of them?'

My sister and I were off the hook.

It's always so funny when my mother tells me stories like this. In my mind, I've always had these notions of myself as a quiet child who always respected adults. In fact, I thought ndandi nyabile (I was dull). Apparently, I was the furthest thing from it.

The cows, the kraal and leadership

B ehind me in the photo on the next page is my grandfather's kraal. Apartheid law did not allow any family to own more than 30 cattle. Next to it is a smaller kraal that we used for sheep.

By the time I was seven, I was a veteran cow herder. We only took the cows and sheep to graze once the dew had subsided. This process is an entire production and a lesson in leadership.

We had to lead them out fast enough, before they populated much of the yard with cow dung. Once they were all out, we led the herd from behind. For boys in the village, this is what leadership was. You led from behind, never the front – otherwise, how do you know when one went astray?

The older and more mature cattle would lead and the rest just followed them. At the back were mothers and calves. The slowest dictated the pace for the rest. When the ones in front start rushing, you had to slow the whole herd down. No cow left behind.

Interestingly, if you had a new cow (maybe it was bought from another village), it always walked on the flank. Jittery and nervous. You always had your eye on it because it was most likely to stray and bolt at the slightest sign of provocation. You had to make sure that you separated it from the bully bulls. All of this from the back.

Standing in front of my grandfather's kraal

When I was roughly six years old, I almost got mauled by a new ox. My older cousins were somehow not around. Since it was new, we had separated it from the rest and let it sleep in a kraal with sheep. We had wrapped a rope around its horns and tied the animal to a pole so it wouldn't jump and escape. There is a gentle whistling sound you make to calm any cow or bull down. You edge slowly towards it and make it lower its horns so that you can throw the rope around them.

One day, I was alone. I whistled and cajoled the ox into lowering its horns. As I was tying the rope around the horns, it picked me up with them and threw me in the air. I landed on the flat horns and it flung me upwards again. I fell on the ground and it was about to stab me with its horns when I rolled away.

The new ox escaped. I had to walk hunched over for months afterwards. Years later, I realised it was probably because I had cracked a rib.

When the village snows

In winter, the beautiful mountains in the photo on the next page are covered in snow and might deceive others into romanticising this place.

It is harsh, hard and unforgiving. I quote myself from my book, *To Quote Myself* (*chuckle*): 'Those who have never truly experienced poverty have romantic ideas about it, and talk about what they perceive as the happiness of the poor. But there is nothing romantic about it for those who live it every day.'

Days like this were horrible. If you were lucky enough to have shoes, you wouldn't wear them, even though you needed them, because they were most likely your only pair and the mud would ruin them. Only the lucky few had gumboots for days like this. And the rest had their bare feet.

Sometimes the smoke from the firewood inside the hut would get so thick, you almost had to crawl inside while squinting your eyes, especially if the wind was blowing the smoke back into the hut.

We would take a long rod of wood (three metres or more) and balance it against the doorframe then put a blanket on it. Which side of the doorframe depended on the direction of the wind. This

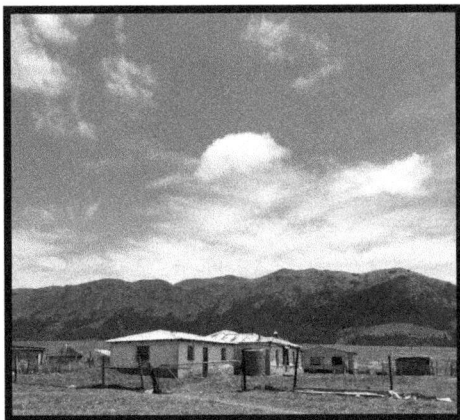

The mountains near Dutyini that can be covered in snow

technique would help get rid of the thick smoke inside the hut. Sometimes the wind would blow your blanket away if it was not tied properly and you would have to run after it and begin the process all over again.

This was the best solution with what was available. You couldn't close the door because of the smoke. You couldn't douse the fire because it was too cold not to have a fire. The life of poverty always gives you unfair choices.

The poor are not poor because they are lazy. They are poor because the choices they have before them are poor options.

My mother and feminism

Even though my mother would not label herself as anything, she is the first real feminist I ever encountered. Hers is a practical feminism, not theoretical. When women weren't supposed to ride horses in her village, she did.

My mother also did not have rules about what boys must do and not do. I used to perm her hair. I think she trusted me more than anyone else to do it right. Ndandimqhuqha nenkwethu (I also removed dandruff from the scalp with a comb). Ukuqhuqha forced you to spend time together. For more than 30 minutes, she would sit on a chair or on the bed and I would stand.

I used to sew and mend clothes. I was taught by my grandmother and my mother made sure I mended my own clothes. I cooked, I cleaned. I polished the stoep. I planted veggies. I kneaded dough. I baked bread. I painted the house. I cut the lawn with garden shears. I uprooted weeds, watered the garden. I carried my siblings on my back. I changed diapers, washed dirty nappies. I put babies to sleep, bathed them, fed them. I fetched water. I herded cows. I played rugby. And when, for a short while, she owned a little shop in Dimbaza, I manned the shop. I could do all those things long before I was 12. All my mother's doing.

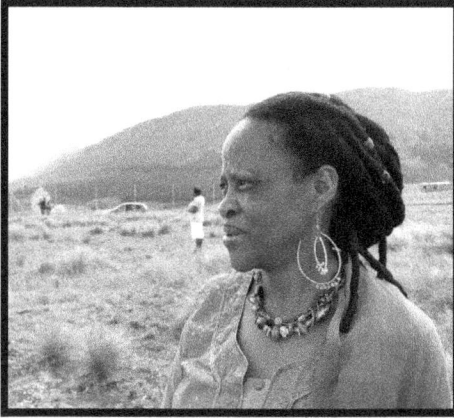

My mother, Nonceba Dlanga

Back in my village, my grandfather had rules about what a boy was allowed and not allowed to do. My grandmother had no such rules but did not want to contradict my grandfather. Even so, when my grandmother wanted me to polish the rondavel with fresh cow dung, my grandfather would never contradict her either. Ndandisinda ngobulongwe as easily as I could milk cows. Nowadays I hardly do any of the above, because I have the means to order takeout and get someone to help clean my place.

Most of my teachers were women. My first two bosses were women. My first and only mentor is a woman. I support feminism probably because of how my mother raised me. Even so, it is still a journey and I am still learning.

Even though women play such strong roles in our lives, our patriarchal society continues to render them invisible and insignificant actors in the 'lives of men'. I don't think that we, as men, truly grasp how deeply sexist we can be. This includes those who are outspoken on women's issues. We often don't stop to think about and question certain behaviours. Simple questions like, 'Would I be treating this person this way if she were another man?' or 'Would I be happy if this was done to me?' can make a big difference.

There are things I have said and written about women that cause me to cringe when I look back. I try to be better each day than I have been in the past.

That time my granddad caught my uncle in the middle of a sexcapade

Every night before going to bed, my grandfather would use one of those reed brooms to sprinkle holy water all over our home while he prayed. The holy water was kept in a 25-litre plastic bucket and had been prayed for by some allegedly holy person. There was a bit of aloe in the water too.

This was a ritual we performed every night after eating dinner, feeding the dogs, and listening to the radio drama by candlelight.

We had several stand-alone houses. There was the rondavel, which was the kitchen (where we cooked with firewood); then the main house, which had the main bedroom, lounge, dining room, guest bedroom and the main kitchen (this one had the wooden stove); then there were also three other stand-alone houses.

My male cousins and I would walk behind my grandfather as he went from house to house, splashing the holy water. Walking behind him was just the smart thing to do. As much as we might have all wanted the Lord's divine protection, no one wanted to be splashed with holy water.

My uncle, Sibongile, who was the fourth-born child, had recently moved from Mdantsane back to Dutyini. He was a charming, kind,

My grandparents' home

funny 24-year-old man, and women were attracted to his city-slicker ways.

One evening, as my grandfather was praying, making it rain with the broom and holy water, we approached my uncle's stand-alone house. I remember feeling tired after a long day of swimming in the river (which my grandmother hated because I would come back ashy).

It was a hot evening and the windows were open. There was a slight breeze that would give relief every now and then but it didn't last long. The lace curtain in my uncle's room danced in the moonlight as the breeze caught it.

My grandfather splashed around the house. Then, out of nowhere, we heard a woman shriek inside the house. Standing outside, we all looked at each other, holding our breath.

We all knew that my uncle had had a beautiful woman in his

stand-alone house for just over a week. She had big permed hair. I had never seen a woman so beautiful in the village before. She had visited him all the way from Mdantsane and had been reduced to hiding in a room in a village.

My grandparents didn't know about this. As decent Christians, it was the sort of thing they would never condone, particularly in their own home.

Now, the splashes of holy water had obviously landed on her through the window and given her a fright.

'He, Sbongile! Ngubani lo ukhalayo apho?' ('Sbongile, who is that in there?') We were greeted by nothing but silence and the mocking moonlight.

'Kwedini, awundi phenduli?' ('Boy, you're not answering me?') Silence.

'I will show you who I am. Makwedini, three of you stand by that window; the other three by that one. Khayalethu, stand behind me.' I had to stand behind him because I was the youngest and smallest. I was seven or eight and my older cousins were in their late teens.

'Nobody gets out of those windows. If anyone tries to escape, beat them with your stick.'

My grandfather was furious, standing by the door, trying to force it open. There was much shouting and the dogs were barking.

After a while, I head commotion near the right window. The girl and my uncle had escaped. They somehow managed to jump out one of the windows and over the yard fence.

My grandfather was even more furious because my cousins had helped my uncle and his girlfriend to escape. They looked up to him;

there was no way they were going to let my grandfather get hold of him. They loved him more than they feared my grandfather, which was remarkable because when my grandfather was asserting his authority, everyone trembled at his voice.

'Nikhamisile makwedini!' ('You're standing there with open mouths, boys!') He turned his whip on them and they ran away in different directions. There was pandemonium. My grandmother came out of the house to find out what was going on. No one could tell her because everyone was running around the yard fleeing the whip. Even though I knew I was free from his rage, I ran for cover.

My grandfather kept talking about how the holy water had revealed the evil that was under his roof.

My uncle was banished from home. Distant family member after family member would come to ask him to forgive his son, but there was no way Kaiser was willing to hear reason on the matter.

In the meantime, my uncle stayed in another relative's home with his girlfriend, where she was free to walk around. But they did live in the constant fear of my grandfather arriving unannounced with his sjambok.

Sunday morning in my village

I took the photo on the next page a few years ago on one of my trips back to my village. It reminded me of my Sunday mornings as a child growing up here.

This image is cute and amusing to me because it's all too familiar. The young boy is faithfully performing his duty – accompanying Granny to church – but he also can't wait to get this walk over and done with so that he can go gallivanting with the other boys.

After waking up on Sunday mornings, I would splash my face, brush my teeth and wash my hands – all with a single cup of water. It was a commodity not to be wasted. I learnt to do this by watching my grandfather.

I would stand before him as he hunched over slightly, with his hands cupped tightly together to make sure that no water escaped his big-ass palms. He would then splash his face and wash.

I had to be careful to pour enough water for him – not too much or too little. He would then take the cup and brush his teeth, and I would stand at attention next to him, ready to grab the cup from him when he was done. He would pass the cup without looking or saying a word and I knew the precise moment to take it. He would

A boy walking his grandmother to church in Dutyini

cup his palms together again to wash his hands with the remaining water. I did the same.

After this, I would go grab his favourite horse, Commando, and with one of my cousins or on my own, I would brush the horse clean. I'd make sure he was spotless, including the tail and mane, and check that he had no horse body salts, hairs stuck together or horse ticks. I would saddle the big, gentle horse and put reins over his head. My grandfather always inspected Commando before riding him.

He would leave for church first since he was an elder and was responsible for the opening of the church. As the lead elder, my grandfather held the keys for the church. My grandmother was the bookkeeper.

My grandmother would follow about 30 minutes later and I often accompanied her halfway. We would chat and she would tell me stories as we walked. The last time I walked with her, before she passed away, I was eight years old.

When I got back home, I ate my porridge, bathed in a shallow basin and got ready for church with my other younger cousins.

The horse I had to chase for three hours

The year after my grandmother, Victoria Boyce, passed away, my mother took me away from Dutyini. My grandfather, Alfred Kaiser Boyce, was not pleased. He feared that leaving the village, going to some private school and spending more time with my mother would make me soft. He was worried that all those years he spent making me a tough village boy would go to waste.

I was nine years old when I left the care of my grandfather to go to a Catholic boarding school called Little Flower Junior Secondary School in Qumbu.

The school forced us to learn to speak English. Before I went to this school, my attempts at speaking English were akin to Willie Madisha mocking Naledi Pandor in parliament. I would also say, 'Hong hong hong hong,' and that was the extent of my English.

At Little Flower, you were given leeway and were allowed to speak Xhosa if you were new to the school and couldn't speak English. You were given three months to learn to speak English only.

By the time the Easter holidays came, my English was pretty decent. About 90 to 100 per cent of my vocabulary was in English. I was so happy with myself.

It was no surprise then that when I went back to Dutyini village, I would ensure that I used my best English. I had to show off.

My sister, Sikelelwa, was eight and I had just turned 10. She was still living in the village with my grandfather and other relatives. When I was talking to my sister, I would 'forget' to speak Xhosa and find myself talking in English. She would just look at me as if to say, 'Really? Do you think I don't know you, negro?' After giving me a look, she would just carry on with something else. I was disappointed. I thought she would be impressed that I was so full of English words that I forgot Xhosa so easily – mid-sentence even.

I would also sometimes pretend I couldn't understand what she was saying to me in Xhosa: 'Can you please say it again in English? I don't understand.'

Once, she replied, 'It's funny how you don't forget that you speak Xhosa when you are talking to Tatomkhulu,' referring to our grandfather. That became awkward really quickly.

My new-found phoniness was not winning me any friends. I thought I no longer needed to go to the veld to look after cows either. My cousins were all out looking after the cattle and I was at home with my sister and other female relatives. When my grandfather arrived in the afternoon on his horse, Commando, and saw that I was not with the other boys, this was a clear sign to him that this new fancy school was making me soft.

He called me over and told me to unbuckle his horse and clean it. Once I'd done that, he made me help him fix some planks on the kraal so that the cattle wouldn't escape. It was a hot-as-hell kind of day.

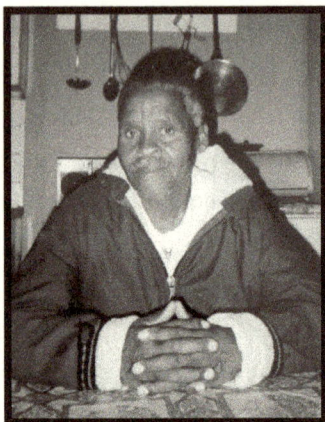

My grandfather, Alfred Kaiser Boyce

One of my aunts called me to the kitchen to eat. Just as I was about to start eating, my grandfather summoned me and I had to run to him again. He pointed to the veld and said, 'Kwedini. Ndiyakubona uba ucinga uba ungumfazi. Uhleli endlini amanye amakhwenkwe esolusa.' ('Boy. I can see you think you're a woman, staying in the house while other boys are herding livestock.')

'Can you see that horse?' Of course I could. 'I need you to fetch that horse – Brant. He is next to those other horses.' It was a good three kilometres away. I was not perturbed because I was used to jogging those kinds of distances. When my grandfather sent us anywhere, he always made sure that we were jogging at a steady pace – simply walking was not allowed. It was no surprise then that I turned out to be a pretty fit kid, even though the current state of my physique, in 2018, may point to the contrary.

I ran out of the main house, the rondavel, past the stable and past a second rondavel, where maze was ground on a grinding rock. It was also a storage facility. The cow ploughs were stored there, along with salt lick for my grandfather's livestock. The sheep and cows would come home on their own when we had a salt lick and you would find them there, licking.

I opened the small gate, closed it behind me and ran, carrying my stick, which was pointing upwards. K, as my grandfather was known throughout the village, made sure that a boy or man always carried his stick with him. A stick was a sign of manliness. You could use it to fend off attacks and troublesome dogs. You were never deterred from going where you were supposed to, because you were always armed.

I ran down the large path that separated my home from that of our neighbours and turned left, running past Uncle Mavela Boyce's house. Uncle Mavela worked in the mines in Johannesburg. He was a loud and gregarious character. He had had an accident while working in the mines and ended up with a stiff neck, which he could never turn. His hair had also begun greying very early. Whenever I ran past his house, he would shout, 'He mtsha' nam!' ('Hey, my nephew!')

I ran past his house and past the gate that all livestock went through from the village. There was a long fence that demarcated a point where houses could not be build. This was where the veld began. Sheep and goats grazed there but the area had been so eroded by grazing and the rains that there were just large patches of dry, hard ground and ever-growing dongas. Fynbos grew all over too.

I carried on running down the grazing part of the veld, which sloped gently towards the river. I went through the river where we often swam and made clay cows and made them fight. I ran up and over the riverbank and stopped at the spring, where the villagers would queue in the mornings and late afternoons to fetch drinking water in buckets. It was midday, so there was no one there. I stopped, bent over and drank from the sweet, cold spring.

When we took the livestock back home, some boys had to stand by the spring to make sure that none of the cattle or sheep drank from it. We would let them drink at the river. The river was also where the women washed clothes every Saturday. They would walk there carrying loads of clothes packed in large enamel basins on their heads. Inside the basins would also be a small bucket or a jug to scoop water. There was also a green Sunlight soap bar and, of course, Omo.

After I'd quenched my thirst on this hot, hot day, I continued running, making my way through the next fence, which separated the grazing area from the fields where the villagers ploughed mealies in season. During the seasons when the villagers weren't growing or planting, the livestock could graze there. This area had longer and thicker grass. After going past the fence, I ran up the inclining veld.

Eventually I got to the horses. Brant was with two other untamed horses. This was going to be tricky. I don't know how I knew that they were untamed but you could pick up on things and just know. This was going to be hell. I knew it. But how much hell was it going to be, I clearly had no idea.

I approached the horses very slowly, cautiously. I did not want to startle the untamed mares because if I did, they would bolt and then so would Brant. I also knew that my grandfather was watching me from a distance back home because parts of the veld were visible from home.

I approached them, hunching slightly with bent knees. I whistled a gentle whistle, with my right hand outstretched and my left hand holding my stick low on the ground. I knew that a raised stick would indicate aggression, and would result in them running away. They continued grazing. I was now about 20 or so metres from them. When I got to about 10 metres, the damn things bolted, as if on cue. They ran for a while, then stopped a long distance from me and began to graze once again.

I had no choice but to run after them. Each time I got close, the horses would bolt. This happened for hours, as if the horses were taunting me. I cried as I chased and ran after them.

Finally, at some point, I managed to get close to Brant. I continued my unobtrusive approach. I didn't want him to be startled. I was in his eyesight. I touched his neck as he was grazing. He continued to graze calmly, but just as I was about to turn his neck to put the rope on him, the wild mares fled and so did he. I cried and cried and ran and cried and ran after them.

After three hours of chasing, I had to think of another tactic. I had to separate him somehow from the mares. When they bolted, they had to run one way, and I had to be in between Brant and them so that he couldn't follow them.

When I finally got back home with Brant, having wiped my tears away, my grandfather looked very pleased with himself. I knew he could see that I was still resilient and hadn't let the city soften me.

How my principal dealt with a white boy who called me kaffir

I was part of the initial influx of black kids who could officially go to white schools towards the end of apartheid. I'd briefly attended Little Flower Junior Secondary School before ending up at Hudson Park Primary School in 1991. I was the only person of colour in my class, and when I first got to the school, white kids were fascinated by my hair.

Being business-minded, I saw this as an opportunity: if they would buy me a pie, chips, or whatever I felt like having that day, I would let them touch my hair. They would often stretch it because they were not used to a black person's hair.

It is strange that we all lived in close proximity to each other and yet were so separated by the system that what should have been normal was fascinating.

While white kids were fascinated by black people's hair, when I was walking in Mdantsane, I would be stopped on the street by grown-ups who were intrigued to see a black child wearing a 'white' school's uniform.

'You go to a white school?'

'Do you mean you actually play with the other white kids?'

'You are not in a separate class?'

'You eat together during breaks?'

'Can you speak English?'

'Okay, speak English then so we can see.'

But not everything about racial integration was amusing. One day, when I was in Standard 5 (Grade 7 to you kids), I was busy writing in my notebook when my boring day changed to one I will never forget. One Portuguese kid kept saying things to me, provoking me. I ignored him. For reasons I do not recall, our teacher was not in the class. The kid wouldn't let up and I wondered if he had been dared by someone else. He was relentless, almost showing off. Eventually, he painted a part of my hand with Tippex.

'Are you trying to be white?'

Again, I ignored him.

Then he said, 'Rub that white off, kaffir!'

When he said that, I lunged at him, jumping over desks to get to him. I had never actually heard that word being used before; I had only seen it in books I had read. One of the books was Alan Paton's *Cry, the Beloved Country*. I knew that it was a word meant to degrade black people. I was raging.

As I went for him, he jumped and ran away from his desk, and some of the other boys held me back. I was furious. I tried to wrestle myself from them but they held me tightly. There was pandemonium in the class.

One boy said to me, 'Don't hit him, because if you do, it's going to be you against all of us. Do you want that?' I was so angry, I had tears in my eyes. I did not care if the whole school ganged up against me at that time.

Then out of nowhere, one kid, Darren, grabbed my arm and marched me out of the classroom, down the stairs. I had no idea what he was doing but I was angry and crying.

Darren said, 'We are going to report him.'

Mr Prentis was the principal of Hudson Park Primary School. He was also my favourite teacher, though he only taught me literature once a week.

Darren knocked on Mr Prentis's door and, before there was an answer, he opened it and pushed me into the office. Awkwardly, Mr Prentis was in a meeting. But when he looked at me and saw my tears, he ended his meeting immediately.

In his plush office, between tears and sniffles, I told him what had happened. He told Darren to bring the other boy into his office right away.

When he arrived, we both faced the principal.

'What did you call Khayalethu?'

'Nothing, sir.'

'Are you calling him a liar?'

Silence.

'Answer me. Are you calling him a liar?'

'No, sir.'

'Do you know what Portuguese people are called when people want to hurt them?'

'Yes, sir,' he replied with the whimper of a scared little boy.

'How would you feel if Khayalethu called you that?'

The boy started to cry.

Then Mr Prentis made us shake hands. That boy and I became

good friends after that.

Looking back, I know that that kid was just trying to gain acceptance and score cool points by doing and saying what he did.

But Darren wouldn't have it. And neither would Mr Prentis.

A list for my mother

To the Queen Mother, thank you:

1. For using a skipping rope in your sixties in front of kids, making them realise it is okay to be playful, no matter what age you are.
2. For giving your children the best shot at a great future, even though all the odds were against you.
3. For dreaming for me, even when I looked at our circumstances and didn't think I could rise above them.
4. For willing yourself away from the jaws of death by asking yourself, 'Who will take care of my kids if I die?'
5. For riding that horse in our village, where no one had ever seen a woman ride a horse.
6. For refusing to know your place because, for you, your place is wherever you want it to be. Even if it's on a horse.
7. For making me cook, clean, knead dough, bake bread, perm your hair, and wash my own clothes.
8. For making me know that being born male didn't make me any better than my sisters.
9. For making me read books. Now I have written books.

My mother skipping rope in her 60s

10. For never asking any of your children when they are getting married or having kids.
11. For just being you. For listening.
12. For not being perfect and not expecting us to be either.
13. For your sense of humour.

Third-World pelvic thrusts and arches

Going to a white school just before the end of apartheid was particularly challenging for black kids because we were still minorities in the school and in the neighbourhoods we walked through to get to these schools. The country was not yet free and it often seemed as though these schools wanted us to know that they were doing us a favour by allowing us in.

Sometimes, our parents seemed to behave the same way too – as if their children were being done a favour: their children were 'so lucky' to find themselves in white schools; they did not have to endure the inferior education that the vast majority of black children had no option but to accept in the townships and villages.

I would sometimes see black kids being shouted at by their parents for speaking Xhosa at home. They wanted their children to get the best possible chances in life and those opportunities came in English. I was fortunate because my mother never made me speak English at home. Xhosa was always the order of the day. English, for her children, was a means to an end; it did not mean we had to shed who we were or where we were from.

But when we were out in town on weekends, she would tell me to go speak to white children. At Little Flower Junior Secondary

School, we were only allowed to speak English and nothing else. So when I started to speak English, my mother would make sure I spoke to white children when I was out, whether we were at the park, the ocean, or the mall – anywhere there were white kids.

'Hambo, thetha nabanye abantwana, aba babelungu.' ('Go talk to the other children, those white ones.') 'Abazokuluma man.' ('They won't bite you.')

I would speak to these children with a great deal of reluctance. Years later, she told me she did this so that I didn't feel like I needed to look at white people with any fear or be in awe of them because they spoke English or were white or had more money. I was just like any child. She was preparing me for a world that was changing fast. Perhaps she could see the inevitability of liberation.

When I attended a white school, I was not in awe of white people, but I was still very aware of white authority. Back in the village in Transkei, authority came with age. Here, authority had more to do with skin colour. In school, all the teachers were white. People who told us what to do, when to do it and how we would be punished if we did not follow orders were always white.

I also began to question superiority and inferiority. Whatever was considered 'less than' was black or from the black world. We left the townships and villages to go to white schools, which came with a better education. We often did not have black teachers at these schools, so the assumption here was that they were not as good … you get the drift.

As schools started to mix in the early 1990s, I remember that black students didn't participate in the talent shows – probably because we didn't know what we were allowed or not allowed to do. But a time came when we finally felt we could contribute.

By then, I was attending Hudson Park High School in East London. At one of these talent shows, I saw free and happy black kids, dressed in their traditional clothes and dancing. They were very well received.

At least that's what I thought.

The following term, when the principal announced that there would be a talent show, the school cheered in excitement. Then he ended off by saying, 'There will be no Third-World pelvic thrusts and arches like last time.'

There were wide-eyed expressions from the black faces in the school hall and a collective inhalation of breath. I turned to my friend, who was sitting next to me. We both looked at each other as if to say, 'Did you also hear the same thing?'

But we said nothing. We simply did not participate in the next talent show. There was no meeting or discussion about it with the school 'authorities', but we kept saying to each other, 'Stop it with those pelvic thrusts and arches.'

There were too few of us. Whatever grievances we had may be listened to in word, but never in action.

A year later, I made a speech at school as part of a public-speaking contest, making the point that Mandela had freed white people even more than he had freed black people. I said, 'We are fighting for your freedom and you don't even know it. We are fighting for your freedom and you are even resisting us. We are giving you an opportunity not to be ashamed of who you are and where you come from any longer. After the elections, all white people will be able to walk anywhere in the world and proudly say that they are South African and Nelson Mandela is their president.'

When we were leaving the hall, the black kids walked up to me and asked if I was trying to get them expelled for saying such things.

It is fascinating how we policed ourselves in that system to ensure that we lived safely. We didn't want to say or do the wrong thing, in case we lost the privilege of proximity to the white world.

Chris Hani and my mother

When Chris Hani was assassinated in 1993, my mother made my sister and I attend our first march. I was young and she had made me very interested in the political situation in South Africa.

She didn't think anyone was too young to fight for rights. Chris Hani had been assassinated and people were angry. Police were all over the townships. The country was on high alert. We were certain there was going to be a civil war.

On that day, I remember my mother saying, 'Today is a very dangerous day. I don't know if we'll die or not but we must go march with the people.' On the way home, back from the toyi-toyi, she said we needed to take different taxis in case the cops decided to fire; she didn't want us to die together.

Only a few months before, in September 1992, Ciskei police, under orders from then leader Oupa Gqozo, opened fire on ANC protesters and massacred 28 people. People my mother knew had been shot at too.

Just because it was dangerous didn't mean we couldn't go, my mother said. Freedom was too close for us to sit and hide in our homes.

My brief career as a pageant boy

When I was about 12 years old, my uncle, Theobold Senzang-akhona Mshumi, was a deacon at a local Anglican church, St Francis, in Mdantsane. He was a well-regarded and respected member of the church, a beloved figure in the community. My uncle was charismatic, and had a connecting beard long before it became fashionable.

Senzangakhona had four daughters: Nobulali, Unathi, Qiqa and Malubekho, and was married to my mother's sister, Nolulama.

Since Senzangakhona and Nolulama had no sons, I had to spend some weekends at their family home to perform some 'boy' duties. As if cutting grass with garden shears at my home all Saturday was not enough, I also had to go to my uncle's place to do the same.

One day, my uncle told my mother that he wanted me to par-ticipate in a fundraiser for the church. However, this fundraiser required me to be, what we called back then, a modla (model). I was to participate and enter Mr St Francis oonobuhle (pageant).

I protested vehemently to my mother. The prospect of parading myself before the whole community terrified me no end. But my uncle, aunt and mother all made the dictatorial decision of forcing me to enter this contest. I had heart palpitations and death wishes the whole week leading up to this hell my family had decided I deserved.

I had just recently moved from the village to join my mother in the bustling township of Mdantsane. Township life and the ways of the sophisticated city were new to me. Granted, I was used to visiting the township during the December holidays for about two weeks, before going back to stay with my grandparents in the village of Dutyini. But as anyone from a village knows, you can't wipe out an entire lifetime of village ways in two weeks.

I had to enter this pageant and learn to walk a certain way. The horror. The only walk I knew was that of a herdboy: walking fast with purpose and no grace whatsoever. My walk had the heavy and determined stomp of someone used to walking without shoes.

My grandfather, Alfred Kaiser Boyce, did not want his grandson to walk without purpose. When he felt that I was walking too slowly after summoning me, he would always shout, 'THENI UHAMBA NJE NGOMFAZI? GIJIMA, KWEDINI!' ('Why are you walking like a woman? Run, boy!') The moment he started shouting, I started running towards him, with my stick pointed up in the air, before he could even finish his sentence.

Now imagine this kid from a rural village who's only used to stomping his feet forcefully. Being part of this pageant was unbearably torturous.

On the day of the event, all the contestants – boys and girls – had to go to the church hall and learn how to walk and where to turn. Finally, the event happened in front of a packed hall. The community had come in their numbers, all paying to raise funds for

My big hair

the church. It was so packed, there was no standing room. It was hot and we were wearing blazers to boot. Wonderful.

How I walked or what I did on stage has forever been erased from my memory. Eventually, it was time to announce Mr St Francis. All 20 or so of us stood in one line. We were all numbered, so there I stood – with a full head of long hair and the number six stuck to my blazer (I had also had a perm and my hair was the envy of many women).

They announced the top five. Annoyingly, I made the cut. Don't get me wrong – as much as I didn't want to win, I also wanted to win. I wanted to win because I didn't want to be a loser. I didn't want it because I could just hear my grandfather's voice back in the village asking, 'KUTHENI UNGENA IINTO ZABAFAZI?' ('Why are you participating in women's things?')

The five of us now had to stand in line in front of this enthusiastic mob. The MC announced the two runners-up. I was neither. I wanted the misery to end.

Then, instead of announcing the winner, the MC asked the packed hall, 'Who do you think won?' Deafening cries of 'NUMBER SIX! NUMBER SIX!' rang through the hall. My heart performed somersaults. There was no doubt that I was the firm favourite. I don't know why.

The MC took hold of his piece of paper and said, 'NUMBER EIGHT!' At that precise moment, I took an unconscious step forward, stepping out of the line. In my mind, the judges would have seen what the audience saw. Then I realised that my number, number six, hadn't been called out. I took a swift, sheepish step backwards.

Anyhow, the winner of Miss St Francis liked me, so I won either way.

I have a sneaking suspicion that my pageant experience is the reason I was selected to judge 2018's Miss South Africa. Right?

My tragic but hilarious Valentine's Day

Every year on Valentine's Day morning, each class at Hudson Park High would take half an hour for people to receive cards and flowers from secret admirers.

The teacher collected all the red, heart-shaped cards and flowers. When it was time to give out the gifts and the teacher read out your name, you would walk to the front to collect whatever it was that you'd got from your secret admirer.

There was always some unspoken competition among the popular kids about who got the most gifts. It was not unusual for someone to walk to the front 15 or 20 times, collecting cards and roses.

Panic would set in if you started noticing that the pile of cards and flowers was being depleted and you still hadn't been called to the front of the class. When your name was eventually called out, there was great relief – you weren't the loser without an admirer.

If you didn't get a card, a teacher would write one for you and pretend to be a secret admirer. We all knew that's what really happened but none of us ever admitted it to each other. We would all get at least one.

The one year, I got a record two cards. Two, fam. It doesn't matter that one may have been from a teacher who felt sorry for me.

One year shall forever remain known as the Valentine-less Year in the annals of Khaya Dlanga. Everyone had gone up to collect cards. Some had gone up 10, 15, 20 times, because they were popular and beautiful and everyone crushed on them. I wasn't popular – but I wasn't unpopular either. When you are popular or unpopular, you are remembered and have some measure of impact. When you are in the middle, you are easy to forget. That was me.

The last card was called out. Obviously, I stood up because it was the last card and I was the only person without one. But as I stood up, someone else's name was called.

I laughed and laughed and laughed and laughed and laughed and collapsed on my chair.

'That's hilarious! I didn't get a card!' Somehow, I found it hilarious. I could see that some girls felt sorry for me.

I was a loner in school who spent all his time in the library. But I actually don't think that was the reason I didn't get a Valentine that year. I blame the hairdo I had that February. Or maybe there was too much month left for the teacher to want to spend money on a card for me.

VIMBA!

My mother had a beautiful, good-quality, heavy camera she used to take pictures of myself and my sister Sikelelwa. She had a knack for picking beautiful, quality objects. Her mantra in life was that you don't need to look poor just because you are struggling. That extended to the kind of camera she bought.

Over the years, I took possession of it slowly. I took pictures of people in Dutyini when I visited but Dutyini had the disadvantage of being in a valley and far away from everything else. This small pool of people knew me and my family and, somehow, that gave some of them the distinct impression that I would take their photographs for free. They were wrong, of course.

I would charge people R2.50 per photo. Since they didn't have their pictures taken that often in the village, there was still great demand for my inelegant picture-taking abilities. People were almost happy with anything and I made a fair bit of money.

During the school holidays, I sometimes went to visit my paternal family in the village of Danti between Mount Ayliff and Kokstad. My grandmother, Patricia Dlanga, was a lot more relaxed than my mother's parents. It also didn't hurt that there were no cattle, sheep or goats to look after. I didn't have to go to the veld to herd any livestock, meaning I had many days of leisure whenever I visited. I would pack my mother's camera and take photos of people, as long as they paid me.

I made a lot of money during school holidays in Danti. The residents there had a little bit more money than the village of Dutyini. Danti is a lot closer to the N2, and this access meant that economic opportunities were better. Dutyini, on the other hand, is very far from the road.

I would always get to Danti with a film roll of 12, and it would take a day or two before the cameral roll was full. I charged each photography customer a deposit. The deposit helped me pay for a taxi to Kokstad, where I went to the CNA to develop the camera roll.

I spent a lot of time walking around aimlessly while I waited for the roll to be developed. I often spoiled myself by buying a Magnum Almond ice cream. After a few hours, I would walk back to the CNA to collect my images. I would always be praying that no pictures were overexposed because that meant I would have to refund a customer their deposit since I had no image to show. The worst thing that could happen was if someone opened the camera and exposed the film before I could develop it.

Once I had collected the pictures, I'd buy a 24-film roll so that I could take double the number of pictures. I'd only need to spend money to go and develop the roll in Kokstad once, meaning there would be more profits for me.

One day, during the school term, I decided to expand my entrepreneurial venture. I took the camera to school to take pictures during break. I wanted to see if I could somehow make some extra money at the school because the kids I went to school with at Hudson Park High School in East London were better off financially. Their parents were high-ranking government civil servants or business people. My mother was neither of those. She just managed to bamboozle people to get us into one of these fancy schools.

I managed to get a few of my schoolmates to agree to have their photographs taken by this enterprising businessman. On my way back from school, I placed the camera inside a pouch on my school bag. This pouch seemed to have been an afterthought during the design process, as if someone said, 'You know what would be great? If we added a pouch for a lunch box.' That's where I put the camera.

I took the taxi from Vincent after school, as usual, to Mdantsane Highway. This place is not to be confused with an actual highway. It is the centre of public transportation for the township of Mdantsane but there is nothing about it that resembles a highway, except maybe the crazy traffic. Mdantsane Highway was always a mass of people coming from somewhere in the afternoons – crowds of people getting off taxis from town to catch other taxis to their respective Units (different sections of Mdantsane).

When I got off the taxi at Mdantsane, I would sometimes catch another taxi when I didn't want to walk too long in the sun or rain, and if I had some money and felt particularly rich. The train cost much less than what taxis did so more often, I took the train.

As my taxi stopped, I could hear the bustle of the street and the taxi conductors shouting. These were the guys who spotted potential riders from a way off and opened the doors for passengers. The taxi conductors' main job was to ensure that everyone in the taxi had paid. Needless to say, these guys obviously stole a bit from their bosses.

I stepped out my taxi and reached my hand behind my school bag. Realising that the camera bulge I had felt five seconds ago was no longer there, my heart skipped a beat. How was this possible and how was I going to explain this to my mother?

I looked around the mass of people pressing against each other, making their way to other taxis, and spotted a fellow wearing a floppy hat typically worn by tsotsis of Mdantsane. I saw him attempting to hide an object that seemed too big for his pockets. I could see that he was trying to act naturally.

I rushed and grabbed him, exclaiming, 'Yicamera yam le!' ('That's my camera!')

'Xolo, ntwana, bendingayazi uba yeyakho.' ('Apologies, little man, I didn't realise it was yours.')

I was beyond perplexed as he slowly handed it back to me. I saw him walk away nonchalantly, disappearing into the crowd that soon swallowed him up.

He was a smart chap because he knew that if I had shouted one word he would have been chased and grabbed, and received swift mob justice. That word was 'VIMBA!' which was code for, 'Catch! Thief!' If someone was chasing another person, everyone knew who to catch. When taxi drivers heard that word, they would stop whatever they were doing, grab their sjamboks and beat the crap out of the thief. No questions asked.

I was glad that I didn't have to explain a stolen camera to my mother. More importantly, had I lost it, I might not have some of the classic throwback pics I have now.

The pregnancy (not mine)

I had the only camera around for kilometres. I had an unbreakable monopoly. But since my village was so small, there were only so many photos I could take, and only so much walking up and down or chilling by the café I could do. Luckily there were other villages I could go to. I walked to these villages with my cousin, Gcobani Dlanga, because he lived in Danti and knew the area and people from neighbouring villages. He is about three years older than me. We hoped to see pretty girls I would be too shy to talk to.

We would wait by shops in those villages because if someone was at the shop, it meant that they had money with them and possibly some change. Not many people ever had the opportunity to have their picture taken. We also waited by these shops in the hope of talking to the shopkeepers' daughters. For some reason, shop-owners' children always seemed really pretty, the prettiest children of any village – followed by those of nurses and teachers. They seemed to have the monopoly on beauty. It was then I realised that money washes people.

One morning, I went to my uncle Bhuti Mthuthuzeli Dlanga's place to wait for Gcobani to finish his chores so that we could go gallivanting with my camera. When I arrived, my uncle told me,

'Kwedini, ndiza kudinga, ungayi ndawo.' (My boy, I will need you, don't go.') Back then, you did not question an adult or attempt to get any more information out of them. You would simply do what you were told, no matter how much it may have inconvenienced your plans.

I asked Gcobani if he knew why my uncle wanted to delay us. He simply shook his head and went on about his chores.

Not long after, I was called into the large, sprawling, thatched-roof rondavel with minimalistic furniture. It was a hot a day, and it was always so cool inside.

When I got in, there were three chairs just beyond the centre. Gcobani and I sat down, with my uncle sitting between us. Nothing was explained.

A minute later, a woman arrived with her teenage daughter, who was about 17 or 18 – about a year or two older than I was at the time.

The teenage girl was holding a newborn baby, wrapped in a blanket. I had questions that I kept to myself.

They sat next to the doorway of the rondavel on grass reed mats. I noticed an immediate tension in the room.

'Molweni,' they greeted.

'Molweni,' we greeted back.

My uncle wasted no time and asked what they were here for.

'Sizise isisu.' ('We have brought a stomach,' would be the direct translation. Which is why they say, 'IsiXhosa asitolikwa,' which ironically means, 'Xhosa is not translated.') I could now tell that the baby was the teenager's daughter.

Drama.

Suddenly, my interest piqued. I shifted in my seat. It dawned on me what was going on. Someone had made this girl pregnant. Obviously, it wasn't me because it would be years before I had sex.

'Why are you bringing it here?' my uncle wanted to know.

'It's Gcobani's,' the young grandmother said while looking down, with her legs tucked under her thighs.

I was enjoying the moment but it was also making me uncomfortable because I didn't know the purpose of my presence in the room. I wanted to ask my uncle if he was sure he wanted me in there but I knew not to interrupt. I also wanted in on the drama that was about to unfold.

When I heard the young grandmother say, 'It's Gcobani's,' I know I must have said to myself, 'Mother fornicator! How has he not told me!' We went everywhere and shared everything together.

'Kutheni umzisa sezele? Ubunga qinisekanga uba ngobani?' ('Why did you bring her after giving birth? Weren't you sure whose baby it would be?') I nearly chocked on the tea I wasn't drinking. Did he just say that? If it were a rap battle, I think there would have been a chorus of 'Oooooos'.

I felt sorry for the grandmother and her daughter. It was a damn cold thing to say. I have an expressive face, I am told, so I wouldn't be surprised if my eyes opened up like the shocked-face emoji.

The young grandmother and her daughter said nothing. The baby in her arms remained asleep.

My uncle turned to a sheepish-looking Gcobani and said, 'Gcobani, uyayazi le ntombi?' ('Gcobani, do you know this girl?')

He looked down and replied, 'Ewe, bhuti.' ('Yes, I do.')

'Hayi ke, buyani kule veki izayo malunga nalo mcimbi.' ('Come back next week, same time, and we will discuss all the terms.')

I was confused because all Gcobani said was that he knew her. Simply saying you know someone can get them pregnant? It was almost a scene from the Bible. 'And they knew each other' – a biblical euphemism for hanky-panky.

I understood what was going on but I was just surprised that was how it was done.

Gcobani did not seem happy. We all left the rondavel. Clearly my uncle already knew that this conversation was going to take place and had already spoken to my cousin about it.

I was never going to be asked to speak because I was a teenager. Only grown men could speak on such occasions. Years later, my uncle told me that he simply wanted me to observe and learn so that if I ever decided to make a baby while I was myself a child, I would know what I would have to go through.

I learnt vocabulary, drama and geography by watching WWF

For me, WWF (now WWE) was very educational. Or I was just a weird kid.

When I lived with my uncle, his house was one of the first houses in the whole of Mdantsane to have a satellite dish. People would often refer to my cousin and I as 'abantwana bakwindlu ine satellite' ('those kids from the house with the satellite').

It was quite a thing for me, moving to my uncle's house. My life took a complete about turn. One moment we had no TV at my mother's house (I was a kid who went next door just to watch the news on the neighbour's TV and then go back home), then all of a sudden, I'd moved to my uncle's house and I had all these TV channels: M-Net, SuperSport, all the SABC channels, and CNN too.

I would get a little irritated by my cousins who wanted to watch WWF when all I wanted to watch was CNN. If I got home and they weren't there, I would switch to CNN and as soon as they arrived, we would watch wrestling because they had taped WrestleMania, King of the Ring, Rumble in the Jungle, SummerSlam and other matches.

I eventually got over myself and began to appreciate it for what it brought us: the drama for them, and for me, education. I first heard the word 'proclivity' (and looked it up in my dictionary) when Vince McMahon was talking to Goldust.

I also enjoyed the writing because I started seeing WWF as soapies for men. When we got back from school, our female cousins would watch *Days of Our Lives* and *The Bold and the Beautiful*, and we would then watch our soapie-wrestling. (Soon, we too became obsessed with *Days of Our Lives*, so when we heard the opening jingle, followed by, 'Like sands through the hourglass, so are the days of our lives,' we would all gather in front of the TV.)

I memorised WWF speeches by wrestlers like Bret 'The Hitman' Hart: 'Madison Square Garden is not a church, but it's holy ground.' Or Steve Austin after beating Jake 'The Snake' Roberts, a religious character, at the King of the Ring: Steve Austin grabbed the mic from the man interviewing him before the question was even asked, saying, 'You talk about your John 3:16, I'll tell you what Austin 3:16 says. Austin 3:16 says, "I just kicked your ass!"' The crowd went wild. That was when I fell in love with WWF because I loved the drama their writers were able to create.

This is also how I learnt which American cities were in which states. When a wrestler was introduced, the announcer would say, 'From San Antonio, Texas, Shawwwwwwwwn Michaels!' or 'From Detroit, Michigan, "Big Daddy Cool" Diesel!' or 'From Miami, Florida, Razor Ramon!'

By the time I was following American elections, when primaries were taking place, I had heard a lot about those cities and states by just watching wrestling. Thank you, WWF wrestling, for teaching me American geography.

My brown shoes and school suspension

The last time my mother was at school with me, she was almost in tears inside the principal's office. I was 17 years old and had been summoned there because my shoes turned out to be brown instead of black.

My old shoes had decided to take a retirement package. I had patched them together many times. Glue could no longer stick them together. But luckily (or unluckily, as the case may be), I had dark-brown shoes.

The brown colour was not school regulation, but since my mother did not work and hadn't worked for years, I did not want to bother her and tell her I had no school shoes. I had three other siblings who needed to go to school as well. Plus, I liked to have food at home. So I wasn't about to jeopardise eating over having black, school-regulation shoes.

One Friday, my black shoes finally gave up and died, so worn out they were not to be worn again. On Sunday, I did what millions of children around the country did back then: I went to the cabinet where we kept the shoe polish, a brush and the Eveready batteries for the radio, since we had no electricity at home. I took the black shoe polish to the red stoep of our four-roomed house, and sat down. My plan was to take my dark-brown shoes and polish them to disguise their true colour.

After I was done, I inspected my brown shoes to make sure that they would not betray me by showing me their true colours. 'I know they say you should show your true colours but tomorrow would not be a good time to do that, shoe,' I said to the shoe. 'Be fake and proud, shoe!'

I avoided playing touch rugby during the break at school even though I desperately wanted to. If I started playing with the other kids, my black shoe polish was likely to smudge. When I got home after school, I would polish them again, ready for the next day.

Over time, I became more confident. I started to play touch rugby during break – carefully though. Which is odd, because the last thing you should do is play touch rugby carefully. Rugby, by nature, is not supposed to be careful.

My confidence came back to bite me in the ass. Big time.

One day, I played touch rugby and my competitive nature took over. I forgot to be careful. When break ended, I looked at my shoes and yep, they showed patches of brown. I decided to add some dust from the field to them so that they would look like they were just dirty. Genius.

Or was it? While I was walking to class, Mr Muller, one of our teachers, noticed my shoes.

'Khayalethu, why are your shoes brown?' he said.

I sir-ed in surprise. 'Sir?' I said, looking at my shoes. Obviously, they were brown. 'I don't know what happened,' I said weakly.

He was uninterested. He sent me to see Mr Friend, the principal, immediately.

Mr Friend told me that I was going to be suspended from school for wearing the wrong shoes, but they needed my mother to be present at the school to give her the reasons for suspending me. I was not sent back to class. I had to wait in the reception area for my mother to arrive.

They wanted to know how she could be contacted. I gave them our neighbour's number. We had no phone at home and were at the mercy of Aunt Nonesi, who was our neighbour. We also kept food that needed to be refrigerated at her house because we had no electricity and therefore no fridge. I used to go watch TV at another neighbour's house.

They called and reached her. She was told that she was needed at the school regarding a matter that involved my suspension. She had to walk to catch a taxi, then travel to Highway to catch a taxi to Vincent. Since it was daytime, the taxis didn't fill up quickly as everyone was at work already. The taxis wouldn't leave until they had 15 passengers, so she had to wait.

She was like many black women: a struggling single mother trying to get her children the best possible education she could not afford. Let's face it – she could not afford it. Yet she did not let that stop her, even though she had been unemployed for about six years. She was always finding a way.

When she arrived, after being summoned all the way from Mdantsane, I could see the terror on her face. She thought I was going to be expelled.

The principal said he could not allow me to come to school while wearing shoes that did not fit the school regulations. I explained that my mother was unemployed and had no money and could not just buy shoes without months of planning. My mother asked him not to suspend me because exams were around the corner. She told him that she would make a plan to get me black shoes.

He would not hear it. I was suspended for the rest of the week.

I ended up buying black shoe dye (my mother's idea) and turning the shoes black. It was significantly cheaper than buying brand-new black ones.

My first kiss – poster child of gwababa

I received my first kiss, under duress, a few days after the picture on the next page was taken. I had just turned 18.

When I was 16, my mother had shipped me off to live with my uncle and his family because she could no longer afford to fend for all of us. There wasn't enough room for everyone since we shared the four-roomed house with another family.

When I moved to my uncle's place in NU 16 in Mdantsane, I had no idea that my days of being a loner were about to end. My cousin, Mncedisi, a month younger than me, was a great extrovert. He wouldn't allow me to be the loner with his nose buried inside a library book or a *Time* or *Newsweek* magazine.

Two days after I had moved there, I stepped outside the house with Mncedisi to get milk at the small local café. I saw something I had never seen before. There were seven girls, all well dressed, standing and leaning against the stop-nonsense in my new neighbour's yard. The girls were between 15 and 17 years old. They just stood there in the morning sun, facing my uncle's house.

'They see fresh meat,' my cousin said, 'and you're it.'

It happened the next day, and the next, and the next. The neighbour who lived at that house was named Asanda and she was very

Celebrating my 18th birthday with the neighbours

pretty. Asanda started talking to us and, later, so did her friends. Suddenly, we were friends with the prettiest girls in the neighbourhood.

Asanda had a stout, shapely build, and a bounce about her walk. She always walked like she was in a hurry to get somewhere.

My cousin had fallen hard for Asanda. He was not the kind to hide his affections very well, whereas she was lukewarm to cold towards him. At times, she would be very dismissive: 'Khandiyeke, man, yintoni kangaka?' ('Leave me alone, man, what's wrong with you?')

Still, he was gentle and extremely affectionate. No matter how rough she was towards him, he was never disheartened. I could tell that she had a slight interest in me but I had no interest in her. I was happily single.

One evening, while we were all watching TV, she arrived and

casually summoned me: 'Khaya, walk me to the shops.'

It was not unusual for her to ask me to walk with her, but while we were walking, out of nowhere, she stopped and kissed me, putting her tongue in my mouth. My tongue was paralysed by this.

When she was done, she carried on talking as if nothing had happened.

We got to the shop and bought bread. We made our way back as if nothing had happened. Then just before we got to our homes, she stopped and kissed me again. I was shaken. Again?

She made her way to her house and I went home, still reeling.

Only a few minutes had passed before she came back and asked me to walk her to the shops a second time. I hesitated, but then my uncle gave me one of his death stares, which moved me to action immediately. He thought I was being rude.

I talked a lot this time, trying to make sure that she would be too distracted by conversation to pull the same trick on me. We went to the same shop and this time we got milk. On the way back, she tried to kiss me again, but I leaned backwards.

'You can't be kissing me, Asanda,' I said.

'Why not?' she asked.

'You are not my girlfriend,' I replied.

She stood in front of me and said, 'Khandi phuze, Khaya. Khandi phuze, Khaya. Khandi phuze. Khandi phuze, Khaya.' ('Kiss me, Khaya. Kiss me, Khaya. Kiss me. Kiss me, Khaya.')

I told her I couldn't and she stormed off towards her house, not looking back. She didn't talk to me for weeks after that.

My matric dance and gwababa 2.0

At my matric dance, my outfit was not the only tragedy. (I wore what one could call a green-cum-beige jacket with a white polo neck. Over it, I had two chains – not the rapper type, obviously, but two necklaces.) Here is how the real tragedy unfolded.

Some years before, I had started taking the train to and from school without my mother knowing. My mother gave me taxi fare every morning but I figured out that if going to school cost R10 per day on the taxi, the train cost me R10 for the whole week. I had R40 in my pocket every week, so the long walk from and to the train was worth it.

After school, before taking the train back from Vincent train station in East London, I would usually go to the CNA at Vincent Park Shopping Centre, a local mall, to read *Superman*, *Spider-Man*, *Jughead*, *Archie*, *Richie Rich*, *Time* magazine, *Scientific American*, *Popular Mechanics* and various other geeky material that ensured I would continue not knowing how to talk to girls. I could never afford to buy any of the magazines so I just read them in the store. Otherwise, I would go to Vincent Library, where I read some more on the planets, cosmos, and art history, as well as novels.

But this day was one of those rare days when I did not go geek out. On this day, I decided to take the train back from school earlier than usual.

I had to wear my red Hudson Park High School blazer in the sweltering sun since we were not allowed to take off our blazers under any circumstances. I got on the train and noticed that it was not as packed as the later trains. This was great because it meant I could sit down.

I then saw the most beautiful girl, sitting with a friend. She was wearing a light-blue skirt and a white shirt. She too was coming from school – Green Point High. My immediate crush was as jolting as an alarm waking you up in the middle of a deep slumber.

Train Crush looked my way and gave me a slight smile. I turned away quickly. Surely she was not smiling at me. I did not want to be presumptuous. This was my standard response back then. I think it still is now.

Anyway. At some point, she walked past me and I felt my heart ripping my ribcage. I worried she could hear it because she looked at me again and smiled, then carried on past me.

Each time the train stopped at a station in Mdantsane, I hoped she wouldn't get off, that she would hop off at the same stop as me. The train eventually ground to a halt at my stop, Fort Jackson. I saw her grab her bags and I could not believe it. I was excited and terrified all at once. I knew myself: I would be glad to see her every day but there was no chance in hell I would dare talk to her. Seeing her more regularly, if I took this earlier train more often, would be both a pleasure and self-imposed torture.

Let me share an example of my terror. One time on the train, my friends threatened to tell another girl I had liked for some time that I liked her if I didn't go up to her. They gave me five minutes. When the time was almost up, I went to her and said, 'Listen, my friends over there want to see if I can talk you. Just pretend we are having a great conversation and I will be out of your hair soon.' She laughed so much that we actually ended up having a conversation. She was laughing until she had to disembark. They were shocked; so was I. How I came up with that line I have no idea but I needed to get myself out of a potentially awkward situation. We became really good friends with that girl. But I digress.

The next day, I made sure to catch the same train and carriage, praying she would be there. As it approached I repeated a prayer. 'Let her be inside. Let her be inside. Let her be inside.' I walked in. There was Train Crush. I saw her talking to someone I knew. I tried to build up some courage to join them. Too shy. Too awkward. Too self-conscious.

Out of nowhere, she walked to me and said, 'Is your name Bhuti kaKhayalethu?' I panicked.

'No, Khayalethu.'

She knew my name. Even if she got it wrong. I stared at her longer than necessary – both out of pure shock that she just talked to me and at how beautiful I thought she was. Her voice sounded like a song I wanted to hear often and I loved how she said 'Khayalethu'. I don't know if I liked *how* she said it or just the fact that she was saying my name.

Strangely enough, we hit it off and started chatting effortlessly. Her name was Yolanda. After that, we were inseparable. We walked from the train station together almost every day.

Soon, we were waiting for each other after school so that we could walk together. Five months on, we were virtually a couple in other people's eyes. I was in a full-blown imaginary romantic relationship with her but the closest I had ever got was maybe touching her hand by accident.

The matric dance was approaching. I was worried that she would say no if I asked her to go with me, and I don't think I would have handled the rejection well.

Mahle Kwababa, who had been my best friend from the first day of high school, was also struggling to find a matric dance date. The girl he had hoped would go with him had declined, and I promised to ask someone for him. That someone was Yolanda, my Train Crush. I badly wanted to ask her to be my date but, no, the coward in me could not.

When I asked her if she would be Mahle's date, she agreed. I don't know if a part of me was hoping she would say no – that she wanted to go with me – or if I'd just wanted her to be there, even if she wasn't going to be with me.

The girl I had asked to be my date decided at the last minute that she couldn't make it as she did not have a dress. God was punishing me for my stupidity.

My family got my cousin, Nobulali Mshumi, who is seven years older than me, to be my date. I wondered if people could tell that I was with my cousin, if they would notice that she was older, and if they would laugh and make fun of me. Fortunately, no one could tell. Nobulali has always looked young for her age, and she is really beautiful, so it seemed like I had scored.

At the dance, Yolanda avoided my friend. He told me he saw her kiss another guy. Years later, she told me she'd been disappointed that I never asked her myself because, 'I had an even bigger crush on you.'

I didn't ask her because I couldn't bear the thought of her saying no. Sometimes we trust what we are afraid of more than what we want. Gwababa.

Hiding my dreadlocks from my mother

From the time I was a teen, I had a love affair, of sorts, with hair. I had a lot of hair too.

When I was at boarding school, there were strict rules about hair. It had to be really, really short. There was no room for self-expression or individuality. During school holidays my mom would perm my hair (that's how I ended up with many Rebecca Malope looks) and she taught me how to perm hers.

I would apply the white creamy chemical to her hair before straightening it with a comb. It had to be separated into perfectly thin rows and it had to be straight before I could put in the rollers. After receiving my mother's training, I could perm hair better than anyone in the house. I was so good that she would refuse to go to people who did it for a living.

During my first year in Cape Town, I started growing dread-locks. In June, I had to go home for the holidays, so when I got to Mdantsane, I wore a hat – I didn't want her to know. Back then, parents tended to think that if you had dreadlocks you were some weed-smoking delinquent, destined for prison. The only thing worse than having dreadlocks was having a tattoo, because that meant you were a Satanist.

Even though it was winter, after a few days, my mother eventually said to me, 'Take that damn hat off. What's wrong with you?'

I removed it slowly, nervously.

'Why are you hiding those? They are really nice,' she said.

I was shocked by her response. I always forget how liberal my mother is.

When I went back home again that December, both my mother and her sister had started growing dreadlocks.

What lobola is and isn't

People who do not understand the concept of lobola seem to think it is about purchasing a wife. There is no such thing as buying a wife.

It's not like a guy goes to Mr Price to pick a woman for the right price so that she can cook and clean.

The original intention of lobola was to create a bond between the two families – that of the bride and of the groom. It was to ensure that the groom kept going back to his bride's family; that he didn't vanish with her once married. In fact, families were never meant to finish off paying lobola, even if you could afford to.

The breakdown of what lobola is meant to mean has a lot to do with lack of understanding, and sometimes greed – families seeing lobola as some form of profiteering.

Often negotiations break down because tempers flare, insults are exchanged, egos are hurt, engagements are called off. The bride and groom have to choose between each other and their families. In the end, what was meant to be the beginning of a lifelong family gathering is broken beyond repair.

Often the argument goes that the daughter was raised well, received a good education, and other such factors, thus justifying the bride 'price'. I don't understand that. Raising a daughter well should not be so she can find a good man; it is so she can be a great human being. An education is to benefit her and society; it is not there to serve her future husband.

Men should stop assuming that lobola makes their wives property to do with what they please. Marriage is not slavery.

Having said that, we also cannot deny the role of patriarchy in what lobola has become. Traditional roles are changing. We need a critical rethinking of how the practice should be applied in the modern era, in order to eradicate abuse.

My Madiba drawing

I had a tough time when I lived in Cape Town, including a bout of homelessness. I was trying to figure out how to make extra money for myself, apart from just being a waiter. Living on tips is difficult because there are no guarantees.

I decided to use a skill I had taught myself when I was in school. I loved to draw people's faces. Specifically, old people's faces. It had become a therapeutic hobby. Using a red pen, I drew the portrait of Mandela shown on the next page. I thought that if I drew Mandela and put it up in a gallery in Cape Town, I could make some money. People would appreciate the difficulty of drawing with a pen, plus this was Mandela's face. In my mind, the picture would be snapped up pretty quickly.

The thing about drawing with a pen is that even if you make a mistake, you have to find a way around it. You have to make the mistake beautiful. The mistake only remains one if you give up. Much like life.

I took the drawing to a gallery in Cape Town, hoping to sell it for R200. The gallery they said it was a good drawing but they were selling a lot of art by street artists and they couldn't guarantee that my work would be sold. I was disappointed by their hesitant faith.

The drawing I did of Madiba, using red pen

In the end, it hung in the gallery for more than three months and no one bought it. I stayed broke.

Eventually, I removed it from the gallery and asked a friend of mine to keep it safe for me. It still hangs in his office in Cape Town.

The toddler who was left alone

One of the most heart-breaking experiences of my life happened when I lived in a house owned by a friendly and rather talkative old lady in Lansdowne, Cape Town.

Aunt Frida was originally from Upington and always had some story to tell about someone or her frustration with something someone had done. Her favourite pastime was to complain about coloured people. (She happened to be coloured too.) They were too rowdy and losing their way. She also loved talking about her white boss, who she said treated her very well.

I would sit in the lounge and nod along to her stories while watching TV and not really listening because she was mostly more interested in what she was saying than in my response.

I also looked forward to her meals from her pressure cooker. When she cooked, she made sure I was fed. I had to enjoy every single ounce of her food. Most of the time, when she was force-feeding me, I was happy about it but there were occasions when she missed the mark and I didn't have the stomach to tell her, as she felt I had a stomach to fill.

Once, her niece, who was in her late twenties, came to visit for the weekend with her toddler. The toddler was about a year old and looked somewhat malnourished.

Aunt Frida started telling her niece that she needs to take better care of her child. I eventually retired to my room to read because the lecturing just went on and on and on.

The next morning, which was a Sunday, I was woken up by the sound of a baby crying. I was immensely irritated.

The child was in the room right next to mine. Her mom was obviously in the kitchen or outside in the garden, where she could not hear the baby. But I was certain Aunt Frida was nearby and would go help.

The toddler kept crying. I suddenly noticed that I could not hear any movement in the house. The TV was not on. No one was walking on the wooden floors.

I started to listen intently. There was no way this baby was left alone. That simply didn't make any sense. I waited a while to make sure, but the sound of the toddler crying was too piercing for no one to hear, even if they were outside.

I peeled my blankets off, hoping I would bump into someone on their way to the room. Nothing of the sort happened. The wailing got louder and louder as I approached the door. I knocked on the door several times and there was no answer. What if something had happened to her mother?

I opened the door to find the child crying all by herself, and I was greeted by the pungent, unappealing stench of urine.

I rushed to Aunt Frida's room. Maybe this is how they teach their children independence, I thought to myself. Sometimes when you are confused by something that does not make sense, you start making up your own reasons, even if they do not make sense either. You don't want to assume the worst of people.

There was no one in Aunt Frida's room. I knew she wasn't at church because she never went to church. I did.

The child had not stopped crying and I went back to her. I felt my eyes well up. I removed the waterproof cover around the cloth nappy and then took off the reeking nappy. The stench of the unchanged diaper was overpowering.

The waterproof cover had done its job and retained the urine, leaving the bed spotless, but the skin around the child's groin had begun to discolour, forming a rash, because she had obviously not been changed all night.

Then I wondered if she had even been fed for her to have only peed and nothing more. It didn't make sense because babies are masters of shit. I concluded that she had not eaten at all last night.

I took her nappy to the bathroom, put some bathwater in a bucket and left it in the water. Then I rummaged through the baby's bag and found other items of clothing and nappies. I bathed her because there was no way she was comfortable. She was crying the whole time. We both were.

My tears were of horror, anger and sorrow for the child. How often was she left alone like this? I was now convinced it happened often.

After the bath, I moisturised, dressed and fed her. She was eating in between sobs. She never turned her face away from the spoon once, as babies sometimes do. Eventually, she stopped crying. I then played with her, trying to make her smile and laugh, and forget what she had been crying about. I did not forget that I was angry, that I was judging her mother. I was done trying to find reasons why she might have left her child all night. All that was left was judgemental anger.

The years of raising my siblings, Sikulo and Nganga, paid off that day. In black families, it takes your older children to raise your younger ones – not a village. I knew exactly what to do because my mother had made sure that it was not the job of a girl to look after children. It wasn't just my sister Sikelelwa's job, or Nomvuyiso's, our cousin. It was mine too. And I was better at taking care of younger siblings than all the girls at home.

The morning passed to afternoon with no sign of the toddler's mother or Aunt Frida. I put her on my back and wrapped her in a towel like I had done hundreds of times with my siblings and various cousins, and she fell asleep.

Aunt Frida arrived back later in the afternoon. She had no idea that her niece had left in the night and abandoned her child. She was furious and started shouting, taking the toddler from me.

When her niece got back from wherever she was, she was hardly sober. I walked out of the living room without even looking at her.

I felt both angry and guilty. I could not understand how it was possible to leave a child on her own for so long. Was this something her mother did all the time? I had an overwhelming sense of helplessness.

My siblings had always been looked after. I'd looked after them, even when I was irritated by it, when I could have been reading or playing. I had also always been looked after. I felt so fortunate never to have had to go through something like that.

Every now and then I find myself wondering how that little girl turned out.

When I was Jesus-zoned

What is the Jesus zone, you ask? Well, I have been a victim and I lived to tell the tale, mercifully. Consider this 'Confessions of the Jesus-zoned', if you will.

Being Jesus-zoned is even more difficult than what has been termed the friend zone. For those who might not know what it is, allow me to educate you: you (as a guy or a woman) find yourself in the friend zone when you're romantically interested in someone, but the object of your affection makes it clear that you are just friends. It is a notoriously difficult area to escape. It is like the mafia – once you are in, you can never get out.

I am yet to meet someone who has braved the Jesus zone and ever made it out of there. Let me tell you the tragic tale of my colossal battle with Christ. Needless to say, I lost. I still want to have a word with Him when I get to heaven. I hope He doesn't make sure I am left outside the club, trying to get bouncer Saint Peter to let me in.

There are few things in life more discouraging than asking someone out and then they give you the 'I'm sorry I can't go out with you because I've found Jesus' line – as if Jesus was lost, hungry, dirty, homeless and malnourished, and now that she has found Him, He needs her to look after Him until He is nursed back to health. Or when they say, 'I'm trying to get my relationship with Jesus in order first.' I think that an honest, 'Dude, I don't want to go out with you' will do. It bruises the ego but at least it's honest.

I, Khaya Dlanga, believe it or not, once got the Jesus line.

There was a young woman I went to church with. She had beautiful, dark skin and an incredibly positive outlook on life. She could even out-smile me – no small feat. Once when I was in high school, a girl walked past me and asked with a disapproving tone, 'Why are you always smiling?' as if I had somehow offended her. I didn't even know I was smiling when she said that to me. I became very self-conscious and tried to stop smiling as much, but a few days later, I had forgotten and was back to smiling again.

Anyway, I had told my friend, Mahle Kwababa, about this girl I liked. We lived in the same house. He knew I liked this woman a lot and I had decided that Friday night would be the night I asked her out.

He drove me to her place and I texted her, letting her know I was on my way to see her. As I got out of Mahle's red Citi Golf, he turned to me to say, 'Chap, even if she turns you down, that door will still be open for you,' in the most serious of tones. We both laughed our lungs out. Perhaps I laughed more than I should have because of a great deal of nervousness.

I walked towards the res and noticed that she was already waiting for me. I was so pleased to see her enthusiasm. She is going to be so thrilled when I ask her out, I thought. She gave me one of her strong, warm hugs. My heart was pounding.

We sat on the wall outside her res at UCT. We engaged in some small talk for a bit. She had just decided to join the Praise and Worship team at church, she said. I congratulated her. In a bid to show her that I, too, was a serious Christian, I mentioned that I had just been made deputy Cell Group leader.

I then could not wait any more so I decided to just blurt it out: 'I wanted to talk to you now because I like you and I just didn't know when to say it because there is never a right time to say something like this.' I don't know where those lines came from, but today, they feel like they could come out of some cheesy teen rom com.

I have no idea what else I said, but I'm pretty sure I couldn't help myself and just rambled on. At some point, I told myself to shut up.

She was looking down. I couldn't tell whether she was shocked because she never saw it coming or because she was trying to contain her excitement about being asked out by the great, short Khaya Dlanga.

There was silence for too many seconds to count. My heart was doing back flips.

'I can't right now,' she said, while looking at her feet. She did not want to see my heartbreak.

'What do you mean, right now?' I asked after a few seconds, because I didn't know what she meant. Did 'right now' mean tomorrow, maybe? Next month, two hours, next year?

'I am focusing on my relationship with Jesus right now. I don't want to be distracted.' She was still looking at her feet. The silence seemed to go on for a long time.

'At least I lost to a better man,' I said to her and laughed.

For the first time since the start of this awkward exchange, she turned her gaze from the floor, looked up and laughed with me.

If you want to be happy, don't resent the people who are

B eware of the poisoned chalice that is umona (envy).
Just be happy for others. No need to find displeasure in their pleasure. You can't be happy if you go around thinking others don't deserve happiness.

I wish you happiness – a lifetime of it. May all the things you do succeed and may you learn to spread happiness everywhere you go.

'You can't date him because he is black'

As someone who was always generally terrified of making any moves that might be mistaken for hitting on a girl, I would often just live comfortably in what some call the friend zone. For many years, I was also celibate, which made things very easy for me. I did not have to try anything. There was no pressure to try to be smooth.

It is no wonder then that I could never tell if someone was interested in me.

When I worked at a restaurant called The River Club in Observatory, Cape Town, I met a beautiful blonde with the deepest blue eyes. We struck up a friendship.

She told me she was working there to save money so that she could go to live and work in London for a year or so. I was working at the restaurant to live – to eat and survive in Cape Town, and to be able to send R50 back home weekly. Which was not much. At all.

The kitchen staff would often tease me, saying, 'That girl likes you a lot.' I would dismiss them as people who wanted to create some drama. 'She told us,' they would say. I still didn't believe them.

We later discovered that we lived in the same suburb. Pinelands. From then on, if we worked the same shift, her mom or dad would pick me up and drop me off. It was perfect. I no longer had to walk to and from work.

One day, when my housemates all happened to be away, she asked if we could watch a movie at my place. I thought that was a terrific idea because I often hired movies and watched them by myself in any case.

Her mother dropped her off at my place and we went to the shopping centre on St Stephen's Road in Pinelands. We hired *As Good as it Gets* – a movie I had already seen and loved. It was funny and romantic. I really wanted her to like it because it would be a validation of my good taste.

We were sitting on the couch, watching the movie when, 10 minutes in, she began to rub her hands together. I found that odd.

She said, 'My hands are cold.'

'Really? It's not cold at all.'

I carried on watching. A good five minutes later, it hit me: Oh my goodness! I think she wants me to hold her hand!

I began to debate with myself. Should I offer her something warm to wear? Get a fleece maybe? Tea or coffee for her hands perhaps? Yes, but what if she wants me to hold her hand? But what if she doesn't? I was dying.

Five minutes later, I braved it out and held her hand. We held hands for the rest of the movie.

Afterwards, we talked about the movie and her plans for going overseas. 'You must come,' she said. I nodded, knowing that was never going to happen.

Before we knew it, it was dark and past 10 pm. Her curfew was

11 pm so I walked her home. It took another 30 minutes to walk to her place, which was close to Howard Shopping Centre in Pinelands.

We talked a lot on the way. When we got to her place, I hugged her goodnight and walked away. I had taken five steps when I felt her hand grab mine, and the next thing I knew, a full-blown kiss was happening and there was silky blonde hair on my forehead.

I was in shock and I was also scared that I could be shot because people still had issues with a black man and a white woman being together.

Still, we started a romantic relationship. In *To Quote Myself*, I mention some of the racial reactions that people had to us during the time we were dating.

One day, a few of us decided to go to the Maynardville Carnival, which happened in a park in Wynberg. Her parents would also be there.

There was much drinking of shots. We ate exotic foods like oysters. We kissed and held hands.

Later, she went to find her friends while I waited in line to get food. She was gone for longer than I thought she should have been and I began to worry. Eventually, I found her friends and asked if they had seen her.

'Yes, we were with her about five, 10 minutes ago and then her mom wanted to talk to her.'

I hung out with the friends and waited. Ten minutes later, I saw her walking towards us, fuming.

'What's wrong?'

'I don't want to talk about it. Sorry, guys, I just want to be with

Khaya now.' I followed her as she stormed off.

We went to get more shots, then she told me, 'My mom saw us kissing and she started shouting at me about how disappointed she was because I go around kissing black boys.'

She told me that she was going to deal with her parents, and then she kissed me. There was not much soberness that night.

I felt terrible for her because I could see how devastated, sad and angry she was. I was not too shocked but I have to admit, I was surprised her mother didn't know about our relationship. Her daughter was spending a lot of time with me. She often dropped her off at my place at night. Did she think we were meeting for prayer group? Come on. Was the mother just proud of the fact that her daughter had a black friend, and did the possibility of a romantic relationship never even cross her mind?

I also thought her parents knew because her father had seen us together. One night, we had been watching movies at her house with her mom upstairs. While we watched the movie on a mattress on the floor, we shared a big duvet and she had her head on my shoulder.

We hadn't heard her dad's car arriving in the driveway, but he walked in, greeted us and went upstairs.

My heart had beaten rather hard when I saw him – not just because I was a black kid in his house, but because she had her head on my shoulder. This was not something I would have been able to do in any black father's house.

Her dad never said anything, nor did he start refusing to drop me at home after fetching us from The River Club.

After the Maynardville incident, her mom wouldn't give me a lift, so she would always insist that her dad picked us up.

Our relationship eventually ended after about a year when she had saved enough money to go to London.

At the time, I was still going strong with my celibacy and I did not intend to end up in another relationship. I was going to be single and live in harmony by myself but, alas, it was not to be. I met a beautiful coloured girl named Sam.

Our relationship ended when she went to London because I was trash. It took me a long time to respond to her letters because I wanted her to dump me. I didn't have the heart to tell her that I was never coming to London.

I think a part of her knew this. In one of the last letters she wrote to me, she said, 'I miss you so much. I wish you could come down here. (Fat chance.) Oh well, met any hot chicks lately? I know you guys are like – all the same.'

A pastor and the 'Thong Song'

One of my great gifts – a superpower, if you will – is my ability to get the lyrics to any song wrong, with absolute confidence.

I had been given a lift by a church youth leader after we had come from a breakfast prayer gathering for men. He was an aspiring pastor named Brendon.

We were chatting with the radio playing in the background when 'Thong Song' by Sisqo came on. It was a massive hit at the time.

'I love this song,' I said as I reached towards the knob and turned the volume up. The soon-to-be pastor looked at me, slightly amused.

'Khaya, do you know what this song says?' he asked.

'Of course I know what this song says.' It was only the most popular song in the world; every human on the planet knew it.

'What does it say?' he asked.

I waited for the chorus to come on so that I could show him how well I knew the song. As if on cue, the chorus made its dramatic break, and I sang along with great lung power.

'Let me sing that soooong! That song, song, song, song, song! Baby, that song, song, song, song, song!'

The aspiring pastor laughed his holy ass off, swerving on the road like a drunk man. I was, of course, bewildered by this crazy behaviour. Since ours was one of those charismatic churches where people would laugh spontaneously in the Spirit, I immediately thought that the Holy Spirit had overtaken him. I figured it wouldn't be too long now before he broke out in tongues. I was wrong.

'Khaya, listen to the song carefully,' he said, still laughing and gasping for air.

I did as commanded. I heard the exact same thing. That song, song, song, song, song.

He burst out laughing again. Tears began streaming down his face and his face turned red. I realised that it might be possible that my superpower had reared its ugly head again but I could still only hear what I had I always heard.

Mercifully, he could control his laughter long enough to tell me the actual lyrics: 'Let me see that thong! That thong, thong, thong, thong, thong.'

All I could think was: what does an aspiring pastor know about thongs?

When I was 21

1. I worked as a waiter because I had dropped out.
2. I had dreadlocks.
3. I was skinnier.
4. I quit working as a waiter, even though I had no other job, because I was starting to think I was destined to be a waiter all my life.
5. One day, I was painting a school when I saw a helicopter crash (they survived). I was interviewed by e.tv's eNews – my first TV appearance.
6. I helped a friend of mine, Chloe, start a magazine and I had the fancy title of marketing manager.
7. I spoke about the magazine in front of 110 schools in the Western Cape, from the richest to the poorest.
8. I spoke at one Afrikaans school in Bellville. When they showed me the hall before assembly, there was an old South African flag hanging on the wall. I was nervous as hell. By the time I went back to speak, the flag had been removed.
9. I dated a white girl and we'd occasionally get racial slurs thrown our way when walking together.

10. I kept a journal, which I sometimes read now to see how I have become worse or better.
11. I had my first bottle of sparkling wine (a cheap one).
12. Under the most extraordinary circumstances, I found a very important suitcase I'd lost the previous year.
13. I lived in a tiny room, which was better than being homeless, as I was the previous year.
14. I took the train every day and I read on the train every day.
15. I read the Bible and I prayed every day.
16. I didn't know I would be where I am today but I was hopeful.
17. I had been through the worst and I was not afraid; it was the beginning of greater things to come.

The war for Sam's cellphone number

My romantic life has had a flair for the undramatic and has been rather uneventful in nature. I am grateful for that.

In 2001, when I began looking for some other form of employment, besides being a waiter, I found out about an organisation called Come and Play. Its role was to go to underserved communities and teach life skills to school kids.

I visited their offices in Salt River in Cape Town, where I met a friendly gentleman by the name of George. After a short and very casual interview, I got the job. George gave me some forms to fill in and a contract to sign. I did not have the necessary documentation so I promised to return to finalise my contract.

A few days later, I went to George's office and found him talking to the most beautiful girl. She had an easy smile, a slim body, and open, gentle face. When she moved her head, her long, dark-brown hair with streaks of light blonde danced. I couldn't believe I was going to be working with such a beautiful woman. God was being insanely nice to me. What did I do to deserve such kindness from the Lord above?

George introduced us to each other – the average-looks guy and the beautiful woman.

'Khaya, Sam. Sam, Khaya.' We shook hands (she continued smiling) and then there was a brief conversation between the two of them. They were obviously very familiar. I didn't want to stand there foolishly but eventually something was said, and I found myself in the middle of the conversation, throwing in a couple of lines that made them laugh.

It turned out that day was Sam's last day at Come and Play. She was just there to collect her last cheque. 'God, really? Are you going to tease me like that?' I said to the Lord.

She left. I was devastated. I turned to George and exclaimed, 'What an incredibly beautiful and nice person.'

He nodded. I then went on and on about her, no longer caring about my application form. Just as I was about to leave, still remarking about how beautiful Sam was, George's landline rang.

'Oh, Sam, what's up?' George said.

I stopped. I was no longer leaving.

They had a brief conversation. While he was on the phone, I picked up a note pad and pen and wrote, 'ASK HER IF I CAN HAVE HER NUMBER.' George smiled and let off an amused chuckle. Looking back, I am shocked by my unusual bout of bravery because gwababa and I are in the same WhatsApp group. In fact, I am the admin of said WhatsApp group.

'Khaya wants to know if I can give him your number,' George said with a little scoff. He thought she would say no.

I wished I had super hearing like Superman then so I could get what was being said on the other end. Instead, I was just standing there, listening to air moving around in the godforsaken local government building.

'Oh? You want me to give it to him?' a perplexed George asked.

I smiled. Maybe I did have a little charm after all. She was not fake-laughing at my stupid jokes. (I was once asked who the most beautiful woman was. 'The one who laughs at all my jokes,' I replied.) George hung up, took my signed papers and started talking to me about the job. After a while, I realised that he was not about to give me Sam's number.

'George, I heard Sam say you can give me her number.'

'Damnit, I don't have it on me now. I will give it to you next time I see you.'

'Oh?'

This was before everyone had a cellphone. I didn't have one and, I told myself and anyone who would listen, I was part of the resistance against cellphones. Now, I look back and laugh very hard at this stance. When I dug deep, not even that deep to be honest, the reality was that I was too broke – not just to have a cellphone but to afford airtime. And so I told everyone I was resisting the encroachment of technology.

George, who was from Mitchells Plain, was a great guy – always laughing, great energy and a really likeable character. I truly enjoyed him but on the next three occasions I met him, he mysteriously still did not have Sam's number.

George was my boss so I couldn't push him too much, but one day I told him I wanted to have a chat with him because he was doing an excellent job of avoiding me. I cornered him in his office and said, 'George, are you going to give me Sam's number or not?

I know that you have access to her details and she specifically said you could give them to me.'

George was silent for a second. 'I will give you her number. I just don't have it with me,' he said.

'I have one question for you, George, and I am only going to ask you this once because you have known her longer than I have,' I said pointedly and courageously to the man who was my boss. 'Do you like Sam?'

There was a long silence.

'I don't know,' George replied.

'Listen, George. I need you to be absolutely clear here. I will ask you again because I actually like you. The only reason I am asking is to give you an opportunity to tell me so that I don't go sabotaging you, if you are interested. Now tell me, George, do you like Sam?'

He remained silent for even longer than the last time. Silence danced awkwardly between us. I was hoping he would not be brave enough to say he liked her but his silence confirmed to me, beyond words, that he really did like her. Eventually his lips moved.

'I don't know,' he said again.

'George, I know I like her and I'm going to do something about it,' I said as I left his office.

I left his office, feeling frustrated. One of the other staff members said to me, 'Why is George being like this? He does have her number, man. He calls her all the time. He even knows it by heart. I can give it to you.'

I couldn't wait for work to end so that I could call her when I got home.

'Sam, hello,' she answered later when I called, her calm, gentle voice on the other end of the line.

'Hi, Sam, it's Khaya. I finally got your number without the help of George.'

We laughed and I told her I had asked George if he liked her. She said she knew George did like her and had, in fact, asked her out. She'd turned him down but they were still friendly. I now understood.

Sam and I began talking on the phone for about three or four months. She lived far away – I was in Pinelands, she was in Delft – so it was very difficult for us to see each other. For a long time, I also wasn't sure if she liked me or not.

That Valentine's Day, I called her just before midnight. My church, the Jubilee Community Church, had an outreach programme at UCT, and I had been there all day and all night. When I called her, the phone rang once and her words were, 'I swear, if you didn't call me today, I was never going to talk to you again.' That's how I knew that she liked me.

When I stopped working for Come and Play, we started dating and I saw her almost every day. Her college was in town and not too far from where I worked at Ogilvy & Mather Rightford Searle-Tripp & Makin, before the name simply changed to Ogilvy. We would meet at the Company's Garden in Cape Town every day at lunch. I occasionally walked the streets of Cape Town with flowers for Sam, keeping a brave face as strange women smiled at me. I used to drop them off at reception for her. She told me how she was always the envy of other girls. (And they say Xhosa men aren't romantic.)

Sam and I were often at the receiving end of long stares from people. I don't know if it was because they thought I must be rich to be with such a beautiful woman (my looks certainly did not justify her going out with me) or if they were trying to figure out what this white woman was doing with a black man. Which was more likely.

One day, we were walking hand in hand in the Cape Town Company's Garden when we felt a warm splat land on us. A bird had deposited a generous helping of crap. I yelped in disgust and she said, 'It's apparently good luck to have a bird crap on you. And it crapped on both of us at the same time.'

I looked at her and said, cheesily, 'You're the lucky one, an average girl like you with such a hunk.' She laughed.

As we sat on a bench in the park (there was kissing involved), an elderly coloured lady walked up to us and said, 'I have been watching you and have seen you in this park a few times. In my day, in fact, not too long ago, you would never see a couple from different races mixing. This gives me so much hope for the future of this country. God bless you, my children.'

We did break up eventually.

Why is the system designed to deprive me for being born into poverty?

In 2017, I was invited by the young and charismatic Mark Sham to speak as one of four speakers at his Suits and Sneakers event. The other speakers were Dr Adriana Marais (a quantum biologist who has been shortlisted as one of the people who will fly to Mars – not to return), Ran Neu-Ner (the co-founder of The Creative Counsel, an agency that was sold for a billion rand – before Ran was 40 years old), and Cal Fussman (Writer at Large for *Esquire* magazine, known for the 'What I've Learned' column). Then there was me. I felt terribly inadequate.

As if that wasn't bad enough, when I got to the Sandton Convention Centre for my talk, I realised that I had completely misheard Mark when he'd said there would be an audience of 300. I was off by another whole zero. There were 3000 people.

When I got up to speak, Dr Adriana Marais had already spoken and so had Ran Neu-Ner. My talk focused on the philosophy of 'first show you can and then ask'. When you've asked for help, people often want to see that you can do what you say you can before they help you. You can't say, 'I am passionate about playing the guitar,' if you have never learnt anything about the instrument. If you can't afford a guitar, you could still try to make one with a tin can, for example.

I used the example of the CV that got me my first job in advertising. I'd had money troubles and had to drop out of college, meaning that I'd left the AAA School of Advertising without any qualification. But since I still loved advertising and wanted to get into the industry, I took a chance and applied for a job at Lowe Bull Calvert Pace – one of the most creative advertising agencies in Cape Town at the time. Everyone wanted to work there. This is what my CV said:

Khaya Dlanga's CV
- ❏ *I live in Pinelands, not Gugulethu*
- ❏ *I can use phones, faxes and computers without breaking them*
- ❏ *Some of my best friends are white*
- ❏ *I can swim (when it's absolutely necessary)*
- ❏ *I am not a member of Cosatu*

Position applying for:
Copywriter

Experience in this field:
I used to write slogans on township walls like, 'Free Mandela' and 'One man one vote'. This was a very successful campaign, as you might have noticed.

I got the job.

It was around this point in my speech that I started to talk about how many black children, even those with natural talent, are not afforded the opportunities because they don't have money to study. I spoke about my creative skills, which fortunately got me hired, even though I didn't have formal qualifications. I was more fortunate than most people in my position. I asked the question, 'Why is the system designed to deprive me for being born into poverty even though I have all the talent in the world?'

A quarter of the room was black and understood the pain of this statement. The other three quarters were white and seemed to be hearing this for the first time. At this point in my speech, the black people in the audience applauded, while the white people shifted uncomfortably.

One white person on Twitter wrote, 'Thoroughly thought-provoking and inspiring until you took it to race.' It showed the great divide in experiences, and more profoundly, the lack of willingness to attempt to understand. To speak about the system as it is, is not an attack on white people but an attack on the system. This is just like the 'men are trash' statement, which is not an attack on individual men, but on the system that men continue to perpetuate, defend and uphold.

I made it clear that it is not just hard work that gets people ahead. It is where they are born and what they have access to, what they are born into. Yes, effort is very important – but that is just one part in the formula for success.

Many people who have 'made it' in life tend to discount how their background helped them to succeed – their great education, or the connections they or their parents have because of where they come from, or the seed money they were given. In my own case, even though I did not come from the most privileged of backgrounds, I was still privileged in the context of my village. I went to good schools; I was given the opportunity to learn English, and – let's not forget this – my proximity to whiteness gave me an advantage too. I was able to converse and connect with white people, who would end up helping me in various ways.

If you are born black, to a poor black family in some township or village, going to varsity after matric will be a luxury and sacrifice for your family. Even if you manage to go, you are likely to drop out because your family has no money for fees and no access to loans either.

This is why corporates looking at candidates should not solely rely on qualifications, but rather look at ability and will too. Undoubtedly, there are professions where formal qualifications are not negotiable, but broadly, the reliance on paper qualifications for many professions will forever condemn black people to poverty.

A retrenchment and an unexpected job offer

While going through an old box, containing my diary and a few other documents, I found my very first letter of employment. I generally don't think of myself as much of a sentimental person, which is why I was surprised to find this letter still intact.

I had been working as an intern at an agency for nine months when I was suddenly retrenched. (I speak about this in my previous book, *To Quote Myself*.) I was earning R2500, which was not a lot at all. I was making less money than I did when I was a waiter, and had just enough for transportation, food and rent. I knew that I had to sacrifice the temporary pleasure of decent money as a waiter for the long-term benefit of getting into advertising and making even more money in future. But now I had no salary and no job in advertising.

Thankfully, the founder of the agency organised an interview for me at a new agency – Ogilvy & Mather. I remember going for my interview in Roeland Street in Cape Town. The building was big and yellow, impressive and intimidating.

My interview was with Greg Burke, an executive creative director. He was drinking coffee and resting his elbow on the table, with his cigarette hand at his ear. His hand moved between his ear and mouth between puffs. No one dared tell him not to smoke. I didn't even think about doing my fake cough. Greg was a legend in advertising, having made some of the most iconic Volkswagen adverts – not just in South Africa but worldwide.

We weren't even five minutes into the interview when I accidentally knocked Greg Burke's cup of coffee over, spilling it all over his desk and onto his clothes. I'd seen the kitchen on the way to his office and ran there to get some paper towels. When I got back, the atmosphere was cold. I was convinced I'd lost any chance of getting the job.

I folded the paper towels and started wiping his desk. It was quickly becoming the world's most awkward interview. As I wiped the coffee from his table, I found myself saying, 'As you can see, I'm really desperate for a job, even if it's a cleaning job.' For the first time, he let out a huge laugh. The awkwardness left the room.

He told me there was a hiring freeze but that he'd look at my portfolio anyway and consider me when the freeze was over. By the end of the interview, he stood up to shake hands and said, 'To hell with it! Rules are meant to be broken. I'm hiring you.'

My new salary was double what I had earned as an intern and I felt like Bill Gates.

When I got hit on by a girl who couldn't hear

In 2005, I was living in Diep River, Cape Town. I always took the train home from work with the romantic notion that I would meet a beautiful girl who would fall for my dashing good looks. But of course, that was never possible because as I got on the train, I would sit down and read my book. If my eyes somehow wandered from the pages and met the eyes of a beautiful girl, I would avert my gaze, looking back to the book as quickly as possible. I'd then kick myself for not making eye contact or smiling back. My head was always buried inside a book, but I'd wonder what it would be like if I actually spoke to someone on the train.

My Fridays had a very specific pattern. I would come home from work on the train, change, eat, finish off a few pages of whatever book I had been reading on the way home, and then leave my place for some party time.

I never made specific plans with anyone. I would just find myself on Long Street and hope I ran into someone I knew. I had three places I would frequent: Jo'burg (which ironically was a club in the middle of Cape Town), The Ivory Room, and Marvel (forever packed with young patrons who would stand and dance on tables). These were popular spots for students and people in the creative world

– designers, musicians, comedians, actors and the like. Whenever I got to Marvel, I would order the same drink: double Jack Daniel's and lime. It would remind me of a great Jack Daniel's billboard I'd seen: 'Enjoyed in fine establishments and questionable joints everywhere'. Marvel was certainly questionable – which is why I loved it.

As I was saying, before I side-tracked myself, I would get home, eat, read, and then walk two minutes to the bus station in Diep River, Cape Town, where I lived.

The last bus arrived at 7 pm. I would always make sure I got to the bus station at least five minutes early because I didn't want to miss it. A part of me felt significantly safer on a bus at that time than I did in a minibus taxi.

One evening, there was a crisp Cape bite in the air, so I donned my blue corduroy matric jersey. (I wore it for years, thinking it was the pinnacle of fashion, which actually exposed my lack of fashion education.) As I walked to the empty bus station with my iPod in my pocket, I felt like the coolest kid in Cape Town. Not only did I have an iPod, but it had video capabilities. I was basically so advanced I could have been on *Star Trek*.

I did not have the money to buy an iPod, let alone a 60 GB device with video capabilities. But back then, I had discovered how easy it was to win a competition if it was exclusively digital.

People did not trust computers so there weren't many entrants. The first online competition I won was for a Motorola V70 mobile phone. You could enter as many times as you wanted. All you had to do was enter your details and say what type of phone was being given away. That was it. You could see how you were ranked compared to other entrants and I was miles ahead. I entered every day because I was using the free internet at my job – every morning, at lunch and before I left work.

I won the phone easily. That was when I realised that I had to specialise in entering digital competitions. Not many people participated and my chances of winning increased exponentially.

So when there was a Bidorbuy competition to win an iPod online, it was a no-brainer …

Back to the bus station. I was always the only person waiting at the bus at that time – but not that evening.

As I approached, I noticed that there was a beautiful coloured girl already waiting for the bus. I didn't want her to think of me as a threat because it was late and I was a man. Well, I still am. I was acutely aware of how dangerous some men can be and did not want her to feel afraid or threatened. I didn't want her thinking I was going to hit on her or rob her, or both.

When I got to the bus shelter, I gave her a quick reassuring-but-unassuming nod and leaned against the left side of the structure. As far away from her as possible. God forbid I speak to her and say something completely embarrassing. I reached into my pocket, removed the iPod and started clicking the circle to change songs. This was probably a tactic for her to see my fancy iPod so that she would be the one to speak to me. I also partially hoped she wouldn't talk to me. All these conflicting emotions in one body.

No sooner had I put the iPod back into my pocket than I felt a tap on my right shoulder. It was the gorgeous coloured woman. She pointed to her ears, asking me what I was listening to. I noticed from the corner of my eye that, in her section of the bus stop, she had a small bag. She was obviously going somewhere for the week-end.

I didn't hear what she said but I (God forgive me) removed the right earphone and started to hand it to her so that she could listen to the music. She quickly signed to me that she could not hear. It was at this point that I wished for a bolt of lightning to strike. God did not answer; instead, He allowed my hell to continue.

I quickly redeemed myself by taking the iPod out of my pocket, showing her the title of the song on the screen. She gave me a thumbs-up. I don't remember what song it was. All I know is that it did not have the word 'Hear' in the title, otherwise I would have thrown myself in front of the bus that was supposed to take me to town.

She started communicating with me while I was still reeling from my state of embarrassment and, somehow, I understood her. She asked me for my name.

'Khaya,' I said.

She mouthed it back. I pointed at her, indicating that I wanted hers. She took out a pen, gently took my hand and wrote her name: Tracy. I still remember how tender her hand was and how the pen moved on my palm. I didn't get struck by lightning, as I'd first hoped, but now, there was a gentle electricity that went through my body. I never knew that it was possible for a ballpoint pen on my skin to feel sexy.

Her touch was different from anyone I have ever met. Each touch seemed to communicate an extraordinary sensuality. I was convinced that she had learnt to communicate with touch in a profound and soulful way that those who can hear are unable to access. Touch was a powerful weapon in her, er, hands.

She told me that she was going to be in trouble with her gran at home because she was getting home late. She didn't know what to do. She asked me where I stayed. I pointed to the flats across the road.

Then things escalated pretty quickly. She put her left hand on my bicep and her head on my shoulder. I panicked. My state of emergency was not visible but my heart started beating furiously. *Why on earth is she so comfortable? I met her less than five minutes ago.* I was also still aware of how beautiful and sensual she was.

She lifted her head off my shoulder and looked into my eyes. She pointed to me, then to herself, then to my apartment building across the road. She then palmed her hands together and put them on the side of her face while tilting her head. She was signing that we go sleep at my place.

I did not skip a beat. I signed a vehement and immediate NO! Then, while committing random, unforgiveable dance moves, I said loudly, 'No, I am going dancing!' She made a sad face.

The bus was approaching. Saved by the bus.

Why did I say no? I was worried that she might have been part of some syndicate that would go to my place and rob my housemates and me blind. What made me think that, I will never know, but that was where my mind went immediately.

The bus arrived and she never got on. I wondered if she really was worried about her gran? Was she going to beat Tracy? Did Tracy come from an abusive home? Was she part of a syndicate? Was she really looking to me as her refuge? If I had agreed to take her to my place, would I have been robbed? Murdered? Would we have had sex? Would I have ended my eighth year of celibacy with this stranger? Did I say no because I was worried that I would not be able to resist her? Or was I more worried about the fact that I only had a single plank-based bed with a sponge mattress?

I must have got off the bus in town, gone to Long Street and eventually ended up at Jo'burg or Marvel as I always did, with her still in my mind.

On Monday, I spoke to my friend and colleague Spike Kunene about my ordeal. He could not believe my actions. He laughed especially hard at how I tried to get her to listen to the iPod and even more so at my reasons for refusing her request.

The greatest pick-up line

When I still worked at The Jupiter Drawing Room in Cape Town, my colleague Jamie Mietz and I worked on a Design Indaba ad. We had met the passionate founder of the Indaba, Ravi Naidoo, and he had told us that design was not just about making things look pretty – it was about contributing to the economy.

During our research, we found out about a designer who had invented a new font that managed to save phonebook companies money. The type was compressed, saving hundreds of pages and making the business more profitable.

The ad Jamie and I made ended up winning a prestigious prize in the gold category and the almost-impossible-to-win Black Eagle Award at the Eagle Print Awards. The winning team won a trip to Cannes – the Oscars of the advertising industry.

When I was in Cannes, I met a lot of people from many different countries, the vast majority of whom were white and male. From what I could see, minorities were astonishingly underrepresented. I take that back: the majority was underrepresented, because most of the world is brown. There weren't many brown people at Cannes, and every single senior person or decision-maker I met was a white man. I was taken aback because I thought this was just a South African problem.

Aside from the serious issues I saw there, I enjoyed meeting new acquaintances. My neighbours happened to be a pair of model-like twins, who worked in Dubai as a copywriter and art director team. I also met a number of women from different countries. There was a Russian, a Colombian, a Croatian and an American. I suspect they felt safer in a group and I too felt comfortable around them. Probably because we were all minorities.

I told them I was from South Africa.

'Do you speak anything else other than English in South Africa?'

'Yes, actually, I am Xhosa speaking. That's my mother tongue,' I said.

'What? Is that the name of the language?' they asked me in disbelief. One of them mentioned that she had seen *The Gods Must be Crazy* and heard those clicking sounds, but she thought they must have been made up.

'Come on, say something so that we know it's true,' said the Russian.

'Qaqambile, likuqale nini iqhakuva emqaleni? Gqhirha iqhakuva emqaleni lindiqale ngoMgqibelo, ndaqonda ukuba mandiqale kuwe.'

They were all laughing uncontrollably by the time I was finished. They asked me to say it again to prove that I wasn't speaking gibberish. I did. They were even more impressed the next time around.

'What does it mean if it's real?'

'Qaqambile is the name of the subject in the story. So here goes: "Qaqambile, when did you notice that you had a pimple in your throat?"

'"Doctor, I noticed on Saturday and I decided to come consult you first."'

There was more giggling as if I had pulled off the world's greatest magic trick.

'I wonder what else you can do with your tongue,' said one of the women.

The Xhosa tongue twister had got me the greatest pick-up line in the world.

To be black often means to be doubted

I was the only black student in my class after white schools were opened to black people after Mandela's release.

I soon noticed that if I got the highest mark for anything, the teacher would be very surprised. You could tell by her tone, which would be equally surprised and patronising as she congratulated me, 'Very well done, Kha'lethu.' (She apparently couldn't pronounce 'Khayalethu'.) 'Very, very well done.'

There was the expectation that the black child wouldn't do well. At best, he should be average. During that era, it was somewhat understandable because older generations had not been exposed to black people as equals. The only black people they had dealt with were their 'maids' and 'garden boys'.

This mentality has found its way to the boardroom in corporate South Africa. I don't know how many times I have been in meetings, where I'm the only black person, and the person presenting looks at everyone in the room but me. And lo and behold, watch their surprise when they realise that the person they have been ignoring all along is the decision-maker.

As a black person in corporate South Africa, before your presence is acknowledged, you must prove that you are good enough. Even though no one does this consciously, black people are presumed inept until proven otherwise. White people, on the other hand, are presumed capable before performing any given task.

But it's not just white people who do this. Black people default to this mindset too. It's assumed that the black person cannot be that important – unless he or she is a government official.

When I worked at an advertising agency in Cape Town, a black man who was about eight years older than me started working at the same agency. He had been there for about a year when my boss asked me to mentor him.

Something interesting started to happen. My mentee would deliberately avoid coming to me to show me his work and he would dismiss my views if I went to help him. He treated me with the greatest disdain I had ever experience from a colleague. Had he been white, I probably would have thought that he was being racist.

I got tired of his attitude, so I invited him to lunch (on me, obviously) so that we could thrash his issue out. I confronted him, and he said the problem was that I was black and so was he.

I asked him whether he had actually considered why I was asked to be his mentor. 'You do know that this was the most awarded agency in Cape Town over the last year?' When he said yes, I asked him if he had also stopped to think about the fact that I had been the most highly awarded person in the agency.

For the first time, the penny dropped.

I had to prove to him that I was good enough before he could accept me, yet he never required that from my white colleagues. He never questioned their competency. Black people doubt other black people. And that is very sad.

To be black means to be doubted. And South Africans of all races do it. We need to grow up and stop it now.

Lisa, ndifuna ukulala nawe

I've known my friend, Lisa Ting Chong, for many years. We first met at an industry event in Cape Town and had a brief chat. She is beautiful and turns heads whenever she goes. Add to that the fact that she is Chinese and there weren't many people of Chinese descent in Cape Town back then ...

The second time I saw her was at a AAA School of Advertising exhibition. When I walked up to her and greeted her, she said, 'You have such a good memory – you remembered me.'

'We only remember what we want to remember,' were my words, sounding ancient and wise. She laughed and blushed a little.

We would become friends, later working together in Cape Town at The Jupiter Drawing Room, where she was a designer and I was a copywriter.

When I found out that I'd won a Cannes Gold, I was on my way to lunch with Lisa, so she witnessed my reaction first-hand.

By that point, Lisa and I were close, so I was glad that she was there when I got this news. To celebrate, she offered to pay for my lunch, and being the traditional man that I am, I absolutely, 100 per cent said, 'Hell yes!' because who says no to a free lunch? Not this guy.

Later, she was working at Saatchi & Saatchi in Cape Town when another friend of mine, who didn't know Lisa personally, got a job at the same agency. I knew that he also had a tremendous crush on her. He could barely talk to her. The industry is small and he always avoided being introduced to her at advertising functions. When he went to work at this new agency, I told him I was going to remove his nervousness around her so that he could focus on his job – because I'm a good friend, of course.

The day before his first day at the agency, I called Lisa. I was feeling particularly mischievous that day. Or that week. Or I have been mischievous all my life. I told Lisa that she needed to impress my friend by greeting him in Xhosa.

Me: Lisa, he will be so surprised if you welcome him in Xhosa.

Lisa: Really? What must I say?

Me: Ndifuna ukulala nawe.

Lisa: Ndifuna ukulala nawe?

Me: Yes.

Lisa: What does it mean?

Me: It means, nice to meet you and welcome.

My plan was set in motion. The next day she went up to his desk, introduced herself and repeated what I had told her to say.

He called me immediately and all I could hear, for a good 30 seconds, was laughter on the other end of the line. I laughed along with him because I knew what had happened.

'You bastard! I knew it was you who'd put her up to it!'

I then got another call from Lisa, who was, thankfully, also laughing.

'Why did his eyes pop out when I said, "Ndifuna uku lala nawe"?'

'Because what you actually said to him is, "I want to sleep with you."'

To this day, when we run into each other, she will jokingly greet me by saying, 'Ndifuna uku lala nawe.' The best part is seeing the reaction from people who understand Xhosa.

A crush and a death

I don't remember when I met her exactly but I know where it was. I was working at The Jupiter Drawing Room, an agency in Cape Town, and she came in as part of The Ripple Effect – an internship programme started by Ross Chowles, the executive creative director and one of the agency's founders.

She had an elegant, feline walk, but she always seemed to be in quite a hurry. I never really got to know where she was hurrying off to. When I finally got to speak to her I realised that her speech was equally hurried but in a gentle manner – the talking of someone who had spent a lifetime being told, by her parents or someone, not to speak too loudly. She had a creative spark though, and the angst was released when she expressed herself in writing.

In those days, we did not have Twitter, Facebook or YouTube to distract us. We had smoke breaks. I am not a smoker but I am restless, with a short attention span. Every 40 minutes, I would take a break to talk to other people in the agency. That was how I got to know a lot of the people I worked with.

One day, I saw her typing on one of the iMacs in the office and I asked her what she was working on. We talked a bit about her work, then I asked her what else inspired her. She told me that she loved to write and she showed me some of her material. I read what she had written. It was then that I saw her for the first time.

Her poetry was simple and hard and painful. There was suffering behind the shy, smiling and slightly seductive Muslim girl. Her depth was visible in the fictitious characters she wrote about.

We quickly became friends and would often talk about books and writing. She would also send me songs she liked so I could listen to them. I suspected that we both began to develop crushes on each other.

The God of Small Things is one of my favourite books of all time and I gave her a copy. It was a book that had been recommended to me by another friend of mine, Ruth Ishumuue. After I'd told Ruth that I stopped reading fiction in high school and was completely over it, she'd dragged me to Exclusive Books in Cavendish Square in Cape Town and showed me snippets of Arundhati Roy's prize-winning novel: 'She was thirty-one. Not old, not young, but a viable die-able age.' The words hit me deep in my soul because they made me realise that any age is a viable age to die – just like my father who was still in his late twenties when he was killed.

She fell in love with the book as much as I had. I continued reading her writing and it continued to intimidate me because of how deeply expressive she was.

One day she wrote me a poem – something no one had done for me before. She called it 'Memory Burn':

> Time is not welcome in our place
> This moment shall never cease

You're woven into the tapestry of my memory
Where you shall echo in eternity
Your name stained upon my lips
Your touch burnt into my skin
I wear you like an etching in my blood
For you will always be with me

I was happy about the poem but wasn't sure how to feel about it because I was an emotional coward then. I read it over and over again. I couldn't believe what the poem said.

Not long after she had written me her poem, I came up with the second poem I had ever written in my life:

We were friends
Maybe not
Maybe more
Maybe less
Maybe between friendship and what would never be
Polite friends
With Polite feelings
And Polite words
Feelings lingered
Dangled
Unsaid
Unspoken
Obvious secrets
Polite friends

With Polite feelings
And Polite words
We smiled
Some secret
Invisible kisses
Never shared
But wished for
Polite friends
With Polite feelings
And Polite words
On Saturdays we saw movies
But really saw each other
We held hands
That were never held
Polite friends
With Polite feelings
And Polite words
'I adore you' we would say
Three polite words
Burying three bolder words
That would never be said
Polite friends
With Polite feelings
And Polite words
You sat on my desk
You wore my shades
You sent me poetry

You wrote me a poem
'I wear you like an etching in my blood
For you will always be with me'
Polite friends
With Polite feelings
And Polite words

There was one day when I believed we would act on our self-restraint. I was leaving for Johannesburg the next day and bidding farewell to the city I had known for 10 years – Cape Town.

We were at the Design Indaba, the world's largest gathering of designers, where we'd been attending various seminars together. During the last session on the very last day of Design Indaba, and my last day in Cape Town, she whispered in my ear and said, 'Please hold my hand.'

I took her hand and her own dug into mine desperately.

I was convinced that she had come to realise that she didn't want me to go to Johannesburg even if she could not tell me. She was using her body language to tell me how she felt. Grabbing my hand like that was a great gesture and made me feel amazing. But it was too late and I had to leave. All the plans were in motion and I was more than ready for Johannesburg. The big city with bright lights was waiting for me and I couldn't stay in Cape Town for anyone.

After squeezing my hand for about 30 minutes, she leaned over and whispered in my ear, over the droning of the speaker, 'Please walk with me. Let's get out.'

We went outside, still holding hands. She walked straight past the toilets, which baffled me because I thought that's where she was heading. We went down the escalators of the Cape Town International Convention Centre, through the rotating door and outside. Still, she said nothing.

I prepared myself for her confession that she had feelings for me. There was an intensity on her face I had never seen before. We left the Convention Centre and crossed the road, and still, she said nothing.

Once we'd crossed the intersection, she asked me to hug her, and I obliged. 'Thank you for holding my hand,' she said. 'I just found out my mother passed away.'

Her mother had been suffering from cancer for some time. I was ashamed of my selfishness, for thinking that she was holding my hand because of me. Meanwhile, she was grieving. When I look back now at those foolish years of my youth, I smile at the comic situation, but cannot separate it from the tragic event of the passing of her mother.

You are already someone

You are already something.

You are already someone.

You are who you are.

You are who you are meant to be.

You are exactly where you need to be.

You are meant to question, wrestle with yourself and the world, until you find your own answer.

You are answerable to your source. Your soul.

You are running your own race.

You are already a winner in your race but you lose when you try to run someone else's.

Enjoy your journey and avoid the temptation of being made miserable by looking at someone else's. They have a different race. They have a different starting point, different equipment, different support and a different personality. What is theirs is theirs and what is yours is yours.

Don't deny yourself the experience of being yourself.

Be inspired by others but only compete against yourself.

You have Wi-Fi on the highway in Africa?

Back in 2006, I was one of very few South Africans who'd started vlogging on YouTube.

I knew that no South Africans were watching the videos because YouTube wasn't a thing in this country back then, but I was something of a curiosity for many American YouTubers. It was shocking to them that I, as a person from Africa, had access to the internet, that I knew what YouTube was, and that I could, well, speak English.

By the standards of the time, my vlogs had a lot of hits. My 120-odd videos had a collection of just over four million views. A number of extremely popular YouTubers had started following me. They would recommend me and I soon amassed a sizeable following to warrant being called a 'YouTube celebrity' by some.

Back then, YouTube would put up a video they liked on the home page. Once that happened, the video was guaranteed hundreds of hits, so it was a huge deal.

One day in February 2007, I woke up to lots of emails congratulating me on being featured on YouTube's front page.

It was Black History Month in America and the featured video was one I'd called 'I Have a YouTube Dream', where I parodied Martin Luther King Jr's famous 'I Have a Dream' speech.

As excited as I was to be featured, there was a lot of racial vitriol being thrown at me in the comments section of the video. Some African-Americans were even upset that I was African and getting so many hits. Many users also found it hard to believe that I really was in Africa.

'Go back to Africa!' was a common expression thought to be an insult. I would respond, simply saying, 'But I am in Africa.'

Around this time, there was a new live-streaming video chat website that had just become popular among YouTubers. I was always getting emails being asked when I would join Stickam. I didn't know what it was but I eventually relented and signed up. It was similar to what Instagram Live is now. You got on camera and everyone else joined your chat via text.

My signature greeting on all my videos was: 'What is occurring, everybody?' So when I logged in to Stickam and joined a popular YouTuber's chat, I typed, 'What is occurring, everybody?'

I received a few responses: 'OMG! Is that the real Khayav?' (My handle was 'Khayav' back then.) 'OMG Khayav! Please open up your Stickam channel so that we can chat to you?'

When I created a channel, one popular YouTuber said, 'I am getting off my Stickam now so that I can listen to you.'

I opened my channel and the responses came on: 'OMG! It really is the real Khayav!' There were hundreds of people chatting to me at a time. They asked a lot of questions.

One morning, I was on my way to work with my cousin, Xolisa. We were still living together then, so we drove together every morning in his BMW 3 series. I would sit in the back, responding to emails, or to comments on YouTube. When I discovered Stickam, I was always on the site on my way to work. Xolisa was completely unbothered that I made him seem like he was my chauffer.

I used my Vodacom dongle on my laptop so I could be online while we were travelling. The first few times I appeared on Stickam while driving, the Americans were what the kids call 'shook'. They could not believe that I was talking to them in a moving car.

'Khayav, do cars in Africa have Wi-Fi? How are you connected to the internet if you're in a car?'

My favourite was: 'Do you guys have Wi-Fi on the highway in Africa? We don't even have that here in America!'

And then I would explain to them that I had an internet dongle connected to my laptop. Many of them didn't even know what that was.

I was surprised that they didn't know what I was talking about but also secretly proud that technology that was standard for many South Africans with internet access was a novelty to Americans back then.

The sister I met once

I have two sisters from my mother: Sikelelwa, known as Siki, and Sikulo, known as Siku. When we found out on my sixth birthday that my father had died, my parents had only had Siki and me. My mother would not remarry. She had a boyfriend, Tununu (also known as Donald), but she did not want to be tied down to a man. She was going to be her own woman without having to be identified as someone's wife. Tununu fathered my other siblings, Sikulo and Nganga.

Nonceba, my mother, has gangster tendencies because she basically told him that the children were not going to be given his surname but that of her late husband. Why? 'Because I'm Nonceba, bitch.' I imagine that's what she probably said.

I don't know when I first heard that I had another sister from my father, Zandisile. He had fathered another child after he left us for Johannesburg to be with another woman. We lived in the Eastern Cape and I would hear that I had a sister in Johannesburg, but she was nothing more than a distant rumour. I imagined she was some glamorous child because she was from Johannesburg. Her grandmother owned and ran a shebeen in Soweto. I figured that she was definitely well off because, in the 1990s, families in the township that owned shebeens generally were. Abantwana base shop.

When I first moved to Johannesburg from Cape Town, I dated a determined, strong-willed and beautiful young woman by the name of Jabu Koapa. I told her that I had a sister living in Soweto and I had never met her. She was surprised that I was okay with it. I had made the mistake of letting her know that my paternal grandmother knew the Soweto address off by heart. Jabu insisted that I call and ask her. Eventually I did and she sent it to me.

Jabu knew I had the address and one day after church, Jabu said to me, 'Khaya, when are you going to see your sister?'

'I just saw my sister in Cape Town last month,' I replied.

'No, I mean the one in Johannesburg,' she said.

I kept quiet. It was all kinds of awkward now because at church they had just preached some fluffy thing about love and reaching out to others so now I felt that I had to say I'd see her that day. I thought to myself, 'Low blow, Jabu. Really low blow.'

'We don't have anything to hurry to after church. I can take you to see her.' Ouch. I had no excuse. I couldn't drive and had no licence either.

'Fine, we can go.' I took out my Nokia cellphone and looked for the address my grandmother had sent me.

Jabu and I eventually got to the address. I did not know what to expect. If my sister's grandmother had owned a shebeen I had figured she must come from a middle-class home.

It was a typical four-roomed house. The gate was closed, and the street was still, with a few people passing by every now and then, which I found unusual for a township. Maybe it was the area. It was 11.30 am.

I was terrified because I had never been to Soweto. All I knew about it was that there were lots of tsotsis. I thought that anybody who looked at me would immediately see that I was not from Soweto – and who knew what would happen to me? Where I came from, Soweto was considered a dangerous place. If you were not killed, you were scammed. My father was killed in this place. He was living here when he was stabbed to death long before he was even 30 years old. That was all knew about it.

Jabu parked the car outside the gate and I asked her to wish me luck. I opened the gate and walked up to the unpainted house. There was no grass on the ground. It was hard clay with tiny pebbles. It looked like there had been a cement driveway many years before but after disintegrating over time, it was all gone.

I stood in front of the typical township house. One, two, three, four rooms. My knuckles knocked on the door. Not too loud, not too soft either. After all, this was Soweto. It was dangerous. It was my first time.

There was no answer. I didn't want to knock too soon after my initial knock. I waited then folded my fist again and knocked. One, two, three, four. The knocking was louder this time but I did not increase the speed with which I knocked. Depending on the nature of the knock, one can detect a sense of urgency, fear, disrespect, or cops. I wanted my knock to remain respectful and anonymous. The knock of an unsure stranger who may be at the wrong house.

No answer again. There was a slight relief. I wouldn't have to deal with this today.

I knocked for a final time. This time, a loud, irritable, sleepy and drunk voice responded: 'Hayi! Ndiyeke! Hamba!' ('Hey! Leave me! Go!')

I did not need to be told twice. I turned and walked away as fast as possible.

But just before I opened the gate, I heard a young woman's voice shout to me. 'Molo!'('Hello!') I turned to look. For the first time, I noticed that there were back rooms, some five metres away from the main house. The door of one of the back rooms was open. This woman looked like she had just woken up as well.

She walked towards me and I towards her. There was recognition in her eyes as I approached her. She was shaking her hands as if getting rid of excess water. 'Ungubani? Ungubhuti?' ('Who are you? Are you my brother?')

The shape of her face reminded me both of my sister, Siki, and my grandmother.

The closer she got, the more I knew she was my sister. Her eyes were Siki's eyes. They were very light brown, almost hazel. Her hair was not completely black, just like my Siki's. She had Siki's complexion too. They both got those features from maMbhele, our grandmother. There was no way of denying the DNA. It did not need to be examined under some microscope. It was apparent.

'Ndigu Khaya,' I said and paused, then I realised I had to say more, 'Dlanga. Khaya Dlanga.' I said it like James Bond but without confidence.

She continue to rid her hands of the imaginary water.

She asked, 'Ungu nyana kaThobile?' ('Are you Thobile's son?')

'Zandisile Dlanga.'

She knew my father as Thobile. Everyone from back home knew him as Zandisile.

'You're my brother,' she said, shaking. She embraced me with her whole being.

I didn't quite know how to receive her. I was still an awkward hugger. And we had just met. I had also heard many theories from relatives and villagers about the murder of my father. His killers were never found.

We started talking outside. I called Jabu to come over and I introduced them. 'She looks like your sister, Siki,' Jabu said.

I now remember that she never invited us inside the house. We stood outside the whole time. She told me that her grandmother had passed on many years ago and the shebeen had long stopped operating. Her mother was married and had left her to live with her uncle. A part of me could tell that she was not living in great conditions. She told me that she had an 11-year-old daughter who lived with her mother. She asked me where I lived.

'Fourways,' I said.

'Fourways. Wow,' she exclaimed in excitement.

'We will come visit every weekend,' she said and started telling me how she would spend her weekends there.

I suddenly had red flags. This is not what I bargained for. I was clearly unprepared for this. All I expected was to meet her and know each other and then take things slowly from there. Everything just seemed to be overtaking me at that point.

'You must see my daughter. She lives with my mother around the corner.'

We got in Jabu's car and went 'around the corner', which ended up being some 20 minutes away.

We finally got around the very-far-around corner. She got out of the car and came back with her daughter, a shy 11-year-old child who did not live with her own mother. A part of me sensed that she was better off living with her grandmother. The conditions were much better with her grandmother. At least from appearances.

'Bulisa umalume wakho.' ('Greet your uncle.')

I greeted the shy child and made small talk. She was holding onto the mother shyly, wondering, I imagine, why these grown-ups were wasting her time.

Again, we were not invited inside, but stood chatting outside. I found it unusual. I figured that was how things were done in Johannesburg. Maybe people didn't trust each other because they might steal. I don't know.

I eventually made an excuse about needing to leave and that's when she said to her daughter, 'Cela imali kumalume.' ('Ask your uncle for money.')

I gave her some money, knowing that the money was not for the daughter but for her. She was asking for herself.

I left, and I was both happy to have met her and unsure at the same time. I felt guilty for not being sure, but my lack of certainty about my sister would be exacerbated over time.

At first, I did not mind giving her money but over time I began to realise that was all I was to her. An ATM. The requests for money were persistent, frequent, and she would use really harsh language. She would then apologise but the cycle would just repeat itself. I felt trapped – she was my sister but I was losing patience. I began to ask myself if she needed help and if I would be abandoning her. Was I a horrible human being?

I had my siblings back home to take care of. I also had my mother to take care of. My other siblings were all still students and I was the only person who was working. My money went to them and towards feeding, clothing and getting me to work.

Her mom lived in a pretty decent home – why wasn't she asking her for money? Was her mom also tired of her?

Was I being judgemental?

I kept questioning myself and the situation.

I called my mother after a few months and told her that I had met this sister. She was devastated. 'Why would you do that? The reason your father died is because he went to that place. He went to them.'

I eventually had an idea. I thought that if I gave this sister my uncle's number (he was in Johannesburg as well), she would leave me alone. I gave her Avukile Dlanga's number and I stopped answering her calls.

A slew of angry SMSes with the most unbelievable insults started to come through. I was mildly impressed by how creative she was in her use of language. Samuel L. Jackson would have been impressed.

After a few months, she stopped sending me texts. I don't know if she had lost her phone or what. My uncle called me months later telling me that all she ever wants is his money and gets angry when he doesn't have any.

I once opened up in an interview on radio about her and I was asked if I regret the decision to cut her off like that. I said no. I do feel guilty but I would still make the same decision.

A heartbreakingly cold moment between a father and son

M y younger brother, Nganga Dlanga, had gone to the bush to be circumcised without telling anybody, and I was incredibly irritated. He was 16 and hadn't even completed his matric. I was aware that he must have felt under pressure to go to the bush because other boys his age were going, but I was the least pleased human being when my mother called me to tell me that Nganga had vanished and gone to be circumcised without letting anyone know or getting permission from his family.

Uzibile. Directly translated, this means 'to steal yourself'. This is not an uncommon practice. Often, boys realise that all their friends are going to the bush, and want to go too. After the ritual, you're supposed to leave your boyish ways behind, including your uncircumcised friends, who are still considered boys. Nganga was young for his grade at school so he had older friends and was probably worried they wouldn't hang out with him any more once they came back from the bush as men.

'Send him a message and let him know he is going to be staying there for a long time. I am not sending money for him to have his ceremony, so he will stay there until I am not mad at him,' I said to my mother.

She said, 'Xolela umntana, Khayalethu.' ('Forgive the child, Khayalethu.')

'I mean it. He is not getting anything from me. It's irresponsible.'

My mother could see my mind was not going to be changed. Three weeks went by and I was still not going to send the money for umgidi (a traditional ceremony to welcome initiates back to the community after they have been circumcised). That month, I sent money home for my mother as I usually did – but no extra money.

To keep up with tradition, she decided to get in touch with Nganga's dad, Tununu, so that he can pay for his ceremony. Many years had gone and he had not raised a finger to help Siku and Nganga. I was the sole bread winner.

'You did not look after or raise these kids. The least you can do is pay for his traditional ceremony. Be a man for once.' My mother told me she scolded him until he was too ashamed not to pay up.

Arrogantly, I had thought that Nganga would stay in the bush for another week or two without my money. I wanted him to stay there by himself as punishment before I would release any money to my mother.

But out of nowhere, my mother told she had the money and that preparations for umgidi were in place. I missed the ceremony because I had commitments at work.

When I eventually made it home to Mdantsane a week later, Nganga was home and dressed as ikwrala (a recent initiate). I gave him a good strong talking to about his behaviour. I had been 18 and had already completed matric when I went to circumcision school, unlike him.

On the day I arrived back, after giving Nganga a strong talking to, a little nine-year-old boy arrived at my mother's door. He was carrying a small bag. At first, we assumed he was a lost child.

The boy said he was from Port Elizabeth and his father was Tununu. His mother knew our address and had told him to come to Mdantsane to be with his dad. He had got on a taxi and travelled all this way by himself.

My mother fed him, and asked him who his mother was and where she was and what she did. I don't remember what the boy said.

His dad – my mother's ex-boyfriend, and father to my two younger siblings – didn't live at my mom's place any more because she had kicked him out. He lived in another Unit in Mdantsane and had gone on to marry another woman.

Nganga and I caught a taxi with the little boy to where Tununu stayed. My brother did not have a good relationship with Tununu and did not want to see his father at all. I told him that he had to, even if this was the last time he would. The little boy was extremely excited. He kept talking about how excited he was to see his father.

'Utatam uzandi khwelisa emotweni yakhe.' ('My father will give me a ride in his car.')

'Utatam uzondithengela impahla.' ('My father is going to buy me clothes.')

He talked a lot about what his father was going to do for him. I've never seen someone so excited to see someone they had never met.

When we got to his place, Tununu was standing outside. I told

Tununu the name of the boy and then gave him the mother's name and mentioned Port Elizabeth.

He looked at the kid and just said, 'Okay,' then carried on talking to me as if I wasn't introducing him to a son he'd never met. The child was a spitting image of him.

Tununu just ignored the boy and carried on talking casually to me, with his fist on his waist. I was broken for the kid. I pulled him towards me and put him in front of me. I put my hands on his shoulders. I realised that Tununu was not going to greet the child. Hug him. Shake his hand. Nothing. He was going to refuse to acknowledge his very existence.

The little boy was looking at his hands, fidgeting.

I looked down at him and said, 'Come, let's go greet ...' I didn't add 'your father', even though I badly wanted to. I figured if I at least forced Tununu to greet the child, he would pay some attention to him.

I walked him up to his dad. Tununu was unmoved. He did nothing. He just stood there. I realised he was not even going to extend his hand.

I looked down and gave the kid a reassuring smile. 'Bulisa ngesandla.' ('Greet him, shake his hand.')

The little boy extended his hand and Tununu eventually did the same. He shook the boy's hand and let go of it quickly.

When I saw he was not engaging, I said to the child, 'Mbuze uba unjani.' ('Ask how he is.')

He asked and got a one-word answer. I realised that I was just prolonging the torture. I quickly made an excuse about why we needed to leave. Much to Nganga's relief.

As we drove home in the taxi, the little boy sat quietly and never said a word.

I told my mother what had happened. She washed him, fed him and gave him Nganga's old clothes. He spent two days with us but he had no money to go back to PE. After the second day, we gave him some money and took him to catch a taxi back to PE.

For a long time, although I assumed the role of provider for the family, I did not want to be a father figure to my siblings – because I wasn't one; I was just a brother.

Once, Nganga, who was visiting me during his holidays, said to me, 'You are the one person I look up to the most.' I felt a massive burden upon me when he said that.

'Don't look up to me. You can't look up to a living person because some time they might disappoint you.'

I was thinking about his own father. I didn't want that responsibility. But when I think about my response now, I wonder if it was cowardly and perhaps cruel to some degree.

Assuming the best

I am somewhat naive when it comes to certain things. I tend to take people at face value and assume the best of them. Not long after I had moved to Johannesburg, I had my first real lesson about not trusting appearances.

In 2008, I had been invited to participate in what was called Highway Africa at Rhodes University in Grahamstown. (Both those names need to change – but I digress.) I was up for The Highway Africa Digital Citizen Award but I didn't know I had been shortlisted until I got there. Anyway, while I was there, I met a beautiful girl who told me she was coming up to Johannesburg for the weekend to visit her family. We promised to meet up.

The next weekend, I was at a braai with my cousin Xolisa when I got a phone call from the girl I had met in Grahamstown. I was surprised that she had called. She wanted to meet up at my place in about an hour, and then head out. She was with friends and they wanted to go to Moloko, a nightclub in Rosebank that has had many names since then.

'Chap, I don't think we need to rush because we are having a good time at this braai,' I said to Xolisa. I didn't really want to stay at the braai. Rather, I was very aware of how little money I had and what time of the month it was. It was just after the 15th and there was a lot of month to go before payday. My heart was telling me that I wanted a Ferrari but my bank account was telling me that all I could afford was taxi fare. I had already resigned myself to staying at this braai. In fact, I thought a better option would be for them to come to the braai.

But Xolisa, wanting to see how beautiful my new Grahamstown acquaintance was, said, 'No, chap, we must say our goodbyes and make our way.'

We got in Xolisa's car and drove home to change into our 'We're going to the club' outfits. They wouldn't let you in if you were too casual. You had to wear a collared shirt, jacket and laced leather shoes. I was determined to resist clubs that required such ridiculousness. But not today.

When I opened the gate for the girl and her friends, a BMW Z4 drove in. I didn't understand how three people were able to fit in a Z4. One of them was in the middle, by the gear box, completely uncomfortable. But they were living their best lives. With the top down.

'Woooooooohooooo! Khayaaaaaaaa!' they screamed as they saw me. Did I mention that while they were driving in with the top down, music was blaring and they were waving around a bottle of champagne? I felt like I was the nerd in a music video who couldn't believe that such people had taken any interest in him. How I did not drop my cellphone when they were on the verge of making doughnuts in the parking lot of the complex is a miraculous event.

I was bewildered. I had been in Johannesburg for just over a year. I was a church-going, Cell-Group-leading, Sunday-School-teaching type, with unkempt dreadlocks. And I enjoyed hanging around the hippies of Melville. This was as far as my 'rebellious' behaviour had gone.

They parked and got out of the car, one of them downing the remaining champagne as she walked over to me. She was a pretty coloured girl and she said to me, 'So you're Khaya,' as she tugged my collar and kissed me on my lips. She was followed by the driver and then the acquaintance I had made in Grahamstown.

As I walked them to the front door, I knew that anything could happen and I was excited, although my Christian sensibilities were shooketh. I had the now-empty bottle of champagne in my hand.

We got inside the house and Xolisa had strategically turned the music up. The driver, wearing a tight-fitting, short black dress, got into the swing of things immediately and after being introduced to Xolisa, she started dancing to the Brandy song. She faced the wall, touched it with her right hand raised high and began gyrating. If we had known twerking then, she demonstrated its grandmother. That would be the more conservative version. I got scared. I might have prayed in tongues, too. I don't know.

They insisted on going to Moloko. I really didn't want to go. Or rather, my wallet didn't. But we soon drove out of our place in Xolisa's car. I didn't have a car. I hadn't even learnt to drive yet.

Allow me an aside here. When I eventually got my own place, I still couldn't drive and had no car. My friends were great enablers of this no-car existence. They always offered to pick me up for one thing or another.

Now, dear reader, please prepare yourself for the most name-dropping-est paragraph in all of South Africa today. I was staying in Douglasdale and Sizwe Dhlomo lived no more than a quick 100-metre walk from me. Xolisa Dyeshana, Poppy Nstongwana, Anele Mdoda all lived in Fourways. They all had cars and were all my chauffeurs.

Trevor Noah lived about 15 kilometres away but Trevor loves driving so he would often be the first one to say he would pick me up when I asked on BBM. (For you kids, BBM stands for BlackBerry Messenger. A BlackBerry is an ancient communications device that took the world by storm. BBM is what predates WhatsApp. Ask your parents.)

One day when I was picked up by my cousin, Hlomla Dandala, the security at my complex asked me, 'Who are you and what do you do? You are always being picked up by these TV people. You must be somebody important.'

I laughed and told him that I am actually a nobody.

Now back to the Z4 people.

We took two cars and my acquaintance from Grahamstown joined us in Xolisa's car because it didn't make sense to have three people in that two-seater car.

As soon as we got out of the gate, the Z4 stopped dead in the middle of the road. Cars were hooting but the Z4 driver did not give a single fornication. We stopped on the side of the road to figure out what had happened. It turned out that she had dropped a lighter.

When we were back to driving, the Z4 followed us. She would keep accelerating and would weave in the road. I was scared for my life and I told Xolisa to slow down and let them lead the way because they were making me very nervous.

After parking our cars underground, we made our long walk to the club. The three girls said we would all be able to get in without paying because they knew some guy. But we got to the door at the club and the door lady was stern-faced.

'We've got stamps,' one of the girls said, trying to walk past her. The door lady shouted at her, 'You go in there without showing me that stamp and I will let my bouncers show you your ass.' Okay, that stopped everyone. They turned back and showed their completely non-existent stamps.

'Get out of my line!' the hostess shouted. Xolisa and I looked at each other in utter confusion.

The girls then held a mini-caucus, as if to elect the chairperson of an ANC branch. Without any communication, they said something to the hostess and then, one by one, they walked in. Xolisa and I figured that the issue had now been resolved, so we followed.

She stopped us, saying, 'The ladies said the guys are paying.'

My face assumed that emoji with the wide-eyed shocked expression.

'Excuse me?' I said.

'They said the guys are paying.' Then, for dramatic effect, 'R60 each.'

This was painful. It was quarter-to-famine time of the month and payday was coming very, very slowly.

'Let's go home, chap. I can't believe they would do this,' I said to Xolisa.

'We're already here, chap. Let's just go in and enjoy ourselves,' he said as he paid his R60 and walked in.

I was now stuck. Should I tell her that I never said I was going to pay for them and tell her to get them out of the club or should I pay for them with my money, which was hanging with desperate claws over a cliff?

I pulled out my debit card and paid while clenching my butt cheeks in absolute anguish. There is a great opening line in the movie *Sin City*: 'She shivers in the wind like the last leaf on a dying tree …' That's what my money was doing. It was shivering like the last leaf on a dying tree.

As we walked in, I said to Xolisa, 'Chap, let's buy our drinks now so that by the time they get back from the bathroom, we have our drinks and they won't bother us.'

He got the first round of ciders. His money was also on its last legs.

I was just thinking, 'Wow, Joburg, wow.'

We drank our ciders pretty quickly because we were reeling from what had just happened. They hadn't come back from the bathroom by the time we had finished our first drink so I immediately ordered two more on my debit card. The total was R56.

'Sorry, sir. You have to spend R100 or more on a debit for us to swipe,' the barman said to me.

'What? No way.'

'It's the policy, sir. I can keep your card here by the bar and you order until you reach the minimum required amount.' In those days, you could do that.

'Fine,' I said as I handed him my card.

We took our drinks and continued our state of depression. When the girls returned, they stood near us and started dancing. I suddenly had a disease that made it impossible for me to see them. My eyes made like Baleka Mbete and said, 'I don't recognise your dancing, comrades.'

They eventually recognised what was going on. We were not about to buy them drinks. I did not even want to talk to them. They moved away and started dancing by themselves.

Later, I ran into Bulelwa, a girl I had met at the braai earlier that evening. We had hit it off.

I stopped feeling so sorry for myself and we all made a night of it. My ego had been bruised and my wallet had been wounded, but I ended up making a lifelong friend in Bulelwa. Sometimes, it still pays to assume the best of people.

My grandfather and his sister

My grandfather, Alfred Kaiser Boyce, and his sister, NoFour Dandala (you might know her grandson, Hlomla), lived three kilometres apart. My grandfather would ride his horse to see her every day. After visiting, my grandfather would always get on his horse in a huff because they had had yet another fight, but he would still go see her again the next day.

I only found out what her real name was 10 years ago, when I went to her funeral. She had been 96 years old. All my life we'd called her Khulu, or by her clan name, maSnama. It never occurred to me to find out if she had a name.

My great-aunt was always old, as far back as I could remember. She always had grey hair, wore glasses and always had a walking stick. She lived in the eSibongiseni compound. It was spacious with many separate houses, and there was a church and a shop within the compound. Her late husband had been a minister and her two sons would also become Methodist ministers. One of those sons is Mvumelwano Dandala, who eventually became a Methodist bishop.

My grandfather was very strict and hated seeing a child doing nothing. He would find something for you to do. Always. Whenever he gave me errands that she thought would be overworking a child,

Khulu would often defend me and they would start arguing.

'This is why these children will be soft. It's because you keep wanting me to treat them like children from the city,' he would complain.

'Leave the child alone. You have been sending this child up and down all day.'

'He is a child and he must learn to work.'

'Hayi, man, K, the child is tired. Leave him alone,' she would respond.

I loved her interventions because it meant less work for me – until I was home alone with my grandfather. He would make extra sure that I had so much to do I would have no time to sit. It was like punishment for his sister's intervention.

My grandfather was 88 when he passed away. Their eldest sibling was rumoured to have been well past 100 when she died. When my grandfather passed away, NoFour became really lonely. She had run out of siblings.

Years later, she was hospitalised in Johannesburg. My cousin Thobeka Dandala (who would later become Makaula) would pick me up and we would go to visit her every day. With pipes all over her face to help her breathe, she was tired and didn't talk much, but Thobeka often speaks about how I would make jokes in the ward and we'd catch her smiling.

She didn't recognise many of the grandchildren who visited. She would always surprise me by remembering me.

'Khayalethu?' she would say.

'Ewe, Khulu.'

'Kutheni uguge kangaka mzukulu wam?' (Why are you so old, my grandchild?)

'Ubu funa ndibe mtsha nje ngawe mhlawumbi?' ('Did you want me to be as youthful as you are?')

'Ngenda yam yeka uK akasebenzise use kanga nje.' ('I should have let your grandfather work you to death, you naughty child.')

She would smile and fall asleep. We all knew her long life was soon coming to an end. We could just sense it.

One day while I was visiting her at the hospital a week before she passed, she said to me: 'You know, my child, I realised my mind was not what it used to be when I asked for my brother a few years ago. I was angry because he had stopped visiting me. I was so angry. Then I was told that he had passed away and that I had been at the funeral. I cannot tell you the pain I felt that day, missing my brother and realising that my mind was also going. I know that it is time for me to go now, to be with my siblings. When you are old and have no one, you just want to go because you are just tired.'

That broke my heart.

I miss them both. And their little squabbles.

Empathy costs nothing

If you don't come from money, you spend an inexhaustible amount of time just catching up. Every step 'the haves' take is a giant leap for you.

Some of my privileged peers have had their parents paying for their rent, apartment, car, education ... Even those who have had to work have still had their parents and their home as a safety net. Many others have no safety nets. We (and God's grace) are our own safety nets.

You can't choose whether you're born into a poor or privileged family, but you can choose how you view and understand wealth in the world. The lack of empathy we have for our fellow men is a terrible affliction. I don't get people who laugh at others for being poor, or snigger at others 'for not being on fleek', when that also costs money. Laughing at someone for being 'broke' probably shows how broken you are. And you probably deserve pity too.

I remember, when I had been working for a few years, a boss of mine asked me, 'What do you do you with your money? Why don't you have a car? You should have one by now.' The tone was already accusatory. He was not asking to understand. He was assuming I was being wasteful with my money.

I never did answer him. I did not tell him that I had a mother who didn't work, and siblings back home who needed to eat and go to school. I could have responded that his children were okay because they had cars he had given them, that his kids did not have to take care of him and his family.

Having said that, I was also privileged where I came from. Our family was probably better off than 95 per cent of the other villagers.

We can't always know where people come from and why they make the choices they make. But it costs nothing to be empathetic and to try to understand.

When I fell asleep next to Thabo Mbeki

I tend to have friends who have an inexplicable affection for me. One of those individuals is none other than Nzinga Qunta, a prominent news reader for the SABC. I had known her for many years.

Despite the fact she accused me of once standing her up (I don't believe it because it's just not in me), Nzinga invited me to be part of a group of young people who would meet former President Thabo Mbeki. It was going to be a small group of 20 or so people.

When we arrived, there was a big square table, and Nzinga and I decided to sit down next to each other because we didn't know anyone else.

A gentleman I recognised (I think the former ambassador to the UN) came up to me, shook my hand, then whispered, 'The president will sit here next to you. Make sure no one takes the seat.'

I immediately panicked. I turned to Nzinga, who was on my left, and told her the news I had just received. I asked that we exchange seats.

She giggled. 'No, Khaya.'

I thought she was joking because who wouldn't want to sit next to a former president and potentially embarrass themselves by saying the wrong things?

I know my propensity for saying the wrong thing at the wrong time and I didn't want this to be one of those occasions. But she refused to switch seats. I tried bribery. I promised to look after her first-born child. I promised her a salary. I even promised her chocolate. Alas, the sister was too principled. As the clock ticked, I became increasingly nervous but I acted as calm as I could.

The president walked in without any fanfare. When we realised he had walked into the room, we all found ourselves standing. He went straight to the chair next to me. I didn't know if I should introduce myself to him or not. While I was still thinking about what to do, he greeted me. I introduced myself nonchalantly. I think.

A part of me was hoping I didn't smell like last night's party – a thought that only occurred just as he sat down.

Let me now recount the actions I had undertaken that resulted in me falling asleep next to the president. A whole president, guys.

I had gone out to party at the residency of the then US Ambassador Donald Gips in Pretoria the night before, which was a Friday. I got home at about 5 am that Saturday. I napped the briefest of naps because my cousin, Xolisa, had organised a birthday breakfast for his girlfriend at the beautiful Fairlawns Hotel in Morningside. It began at the crazy and ungodly hour of 7am.

Miraculously, I woke up, showered, got dressed and made it on time.

He had also organised some outlandish activity after the breakfast. It was some timed obstacle course. I couldn't believe it. I had hardly slept and my head was unforgiving. There was no consideration for those of us who had been living our best lives the night before.

I was very competitive, even in that state, for reasons I cannot fathom. I managed to finish the obstacle course 20 minutes before anyone else. It was not so much that I was fit or faster; I just didn't want to be late for the president. I suspect everyone else took their time because they had nowhere else to go.

It was hot and I was sweating.

I rushed home and showered (again), before picking up Nzinga. We drove together to the Mbeki Foundation. I was excited to meet the man. She knew I was a big fan.

So when I sat next to him that day, I had the previous night's party and the physical activities of the morning deeply rooted in my mind. The president briefly began to chat to me. I don't recall what we spoke about. All I was thinking was that I hoped my gum was masking last night's indulgent beverages. And that I wasn't chewing my gum too vigorously.

After awkwardly trying to appear calm, I took out my iPad and placed it in front of me. iPads were still very new then. As a massive Apple fan, I was one of the first people to get myself one. It had been available for about a week or so. I turned it on, thinking that the president was going to be impressed by this device and we could talk about it.

He leaned closer to me and asked, 'What is that?'

'It's an iPad,' I said proudly because I had something he didn't know about.

'What does it do?' he asked.

'It does a whole lot of things.' I tried to explain and show at the same time. I don't think I did a great job. He nodded several times.

'What are you going to do with it now?'

'I just want to take notes,' I replied.

'Don't do that,' he said in a fatherly way, with a smile.

I felt like a child who wants to show off something no other child in the village has when visitors come around. Like roller skates – you start showing off and skating so that the visitors can admire and applaud you for your ability to glide on the grind. Then your mom walks in and scolds you, tells you to take those things off. Yes. Thabo Mbeki brought back memories that were hidden in the recesses of my mind.

I sheepishly put the iPad away. I was clearly not thinking about things. I was sitting right next to him, and here I was thinking I was going to be typing while he spoke next to me. It was going to be a ridiculous distraction.

When he started speaking, he was fascinating. As captivated as I was though, I had partied the night before, hardly slept, undertaken some gruelling physical activity and now I had to listen to a speech.

The laws of nature defied any excitement or fascination I felt. I felt sleep encroaching and I fought it as much as I could: pinched myself, widened my eyes, clenched my teeth, shifted around in my seat.

I still nodded off. Nzinga had to keep nudging me. Oh, how the mighty slept.

The president continued speaking and never made me feel awkward, even afterwards. I think I did redeem myself by making a few pertinent points and the president nodded profusely.

But I am still one of few people who has slept next to a president in public.

I have shared this embarrassing moment with many people. I told the story to one of my friends, Rose. It turns out Rose then devised a plan. She borrowed my copy of *A Dream Deferred*, saying she wanted to read it. I told her to look after it because I terrorise people who don't return my books.

After a few weeks, to my relief, she returned my book. She gave it to me very nonchalantly and as I was about to put it away on the shelf, she stopped me and told me to have a look at the first page of the book. 'I noticed something inside I found odd,' she said.

I opened it quickly, expecting a torn or coffee-stained page.

Inside was a handwritten note that was not there before. It was signed by Thabo Mbeki. And there was a hashtag, #DontDoThat.

She had tracked down Thabo Mbeki's office and told him that I had fallen asleep next to him and that he had also said to me, 'Don't do that.'

Best birthday present ever.

My friend, the Facebook novice

A fellow I once worked with at the advertising agency Metro-politanRepublic finally decided to join the real world – by registering on Facebook. He had always criticised everyone who was on it, but began to realise that the inside jokes and online references were increasing and he was often left out of them. The thing about an inside joke or an internet meme is that it's not funny when you have to explain it.

When he announced that he wanted to sign up for a Facebook account, I gladly showed him the ropes. I enjoyed the fact that the outside critic was now becoming a member.

A few days after I had been his teacher of technology, he burst into my office, almost out of breath. He was so excited he could not contain himself. I was so startled that I spilled my wonderfully calming rooibos tea all over myself.

He tried to talk and the words were just not coming out. Usually, he was an extremely eloquent and controlled chap. He was measured. But not on this day. No wonder I spilled tea all over myself. I told him to take a moment and breathe. I even went to the water cooler to get him something to drink, though I worried that he would squeeze the hell out of the poor paper cup.

He didn't spill the water, but he gulped it down so enthusiastically that some of it came out of the corner of his mouth. It was at this point that I realised that attempting to calm him down was an exercise in futility.

He placed his palms flat on my desk, leaned over and opened his mouth, revealing a huge, toothy smile.

He then burst out with, 'Facebook wants to know what I'm doing right now!' He didn't so much say this as shout the words in the general direction of my face.

He clearly thought the Facebook prompt (which at the time was, 'What are you doing right now?') was directed only at him.

I tried hard not to laugh and burst his bubble. But I did. Hard. And loud. Months later, I was still laughing at the thought. And now, a few years later, I am still laughing.

Talking about race is not controversial

It is not controversial to talk about race. What is controversial is avoiding the subject and pretending it does not exist.

One of my biggest gripes about South Africa today is some white people who say that we should not talk about the past. In reality, the past still affects us. It lives with us everywhere and every day. The ever-present past.

When I've written columns that discuss race and how it affects those who still have to endure subtle forms of racism, I always get comments that attempt to shut me down. One of my favourite comments is: 'You're so obsessed with race. I don't even see colour. I just see people.' But you can't tell me you don't see colour when you only have friends who look like you and you only hang out in places with people who look like you.

I've noticed that no black person has ever commented on my columns to complain about my obsession with race. It's made me wonder why I get that sort of comment from a white person. Why is it that black people are always more than willing to discuss the topic openly, while a lot of white people tend to avoid it altogether?

Black South Africans are not just generally the ones who're more open to talking about racial issues; they have also made more effort

in integrating. They are the ones who've moved in to white suburbs, learnt to speak English and Afrikaans, and come to understand
Western culture and etiquette. This may be hard for some people to
admit, but black people have tended to bend over backwards to fit
into Western culture and Western 'rules', while white people have not
made a similar effort with African culture. Why? Because there is a
perception that African culture is backward, barbaric and uncivilised.

Some like to argue class, but that is not true either. If black people
in a wealthy neighbourhood decide to have traditional ceremony at
their house, it won't take long before the colour fingers are pointed.

To be fair, this is something that has happened with financially
dominant and militarily superior cultures throughout history – from
the Greeks to the Romans, Genghis Khan to Shaka Zulu. In these
contexts, cultures were assimilated into the victor's way of life.
Today, the world celebrates American culture. We cannot deny its
power and influence – from the hot dog to hip-hop.

Looking at South Africa, where we've adopted Western culture,
the question needs to be asked: did we really achieve a victory in
1994 if we do not fully integrate our Africanness as a country into
everyday society?

It should be no surprise then that black people are more willing to discuss these issues. They feel they have to do more to be
accepted according to Western standards, whereas a white person
will be accepted regardless of their lack of knowledge of African
culture. In fact, when white people make any effort to speak isiX-
hosa or isiZulu, we applaud them, thrilled they've tried. Yet, when
a black person makes a mistake in English, they are perceived as

stupid, even when they speak the language fluently. And yes, even black people judge other black people.

So, I've been accused of being obsessed with race – and that's fine with me. What I am obsessed with is facing the racial issues we have in South Africa so that we can really move forward.

When I introduced Paul Kagame as the president of Nigeria – to his face

I seem to have a skill for embarrassing myself around presidents – a skill I have unintentionally mastered.

I had received an invitation from Google to interview Rwanda's President Paul Kagame in 2011 because I had developed a bit of a following on YouTube, where I occasionally discussed politics. In fact, a few years earlier, when then Senator Barack Obama was running to be the Democratic Party's presidential candidate, I had received an email from YouTube. Obama would be visiting their offices, and they wanted YouTubers to ask him questions. I was to be the one of them.

My question to him started like this: 'Barack, is it okay if I call you Barack?' He laughed. That's the important bit. The rest of the question doesn't matter as much as the fact that I made the future president of the United States laugh.

Now, in 2011, I was flown to Rwanda from Johannesburg, transferring in Nairobi to Bujumbura, and then Bujumbura to Kigali. My flight from Nairobi was odd. My seat happened to be the last one that could be occupied. All the seats in the rows behind mine had all been laid flat. I paid no mind to it except that it was something I had never seen before. When we landed at Bujumbura International

Airport, we did not disembark. The door at the back of the plane was opened. I heard some commotion, as if people were carrying a heavy object. There was much heaving and clanking. Finally, I saw what this was. There was a bed being taken through the back of the plane. This was when I began asking myself questions:

'What the hell? Is that a hospital bed? No way! There is a person in it? Oh my God! There is! Is that a goddamn drip? It's a drip and it's attached to his face! Oxygen mask? He is wearing an oxygen mask! Are they going to take him off the bed or … Oh my God, that's why these chairs are flat. They are putting the bed down on them. Right behind me!'

The nurses, along with the stewards, fussed and strapped him up to make sure he didn't somehow fall off – which was good, because I didn't know if I had the moral fortitude to grab him and pull him up. I didn't worry too much after I saw the nurses. I wouldn't have to do anything, I reassured myself.

It was not long before my false hopes were dashed and I had another conversation with myself:

'No! Are the nurses leaving him? They are probably going to fetch something they forgot. Surely. Wait, are they closing the door without the nurses being here? They are closing the doors and the nurses aren't here! Lord, no!'

The doors closed with an authoritative finality. I caught a glimpse of the man. He was wasting away. He wheezed and coughed weakly. I worried about what he might have. I mean, it's natural to wonder. I did not look back again.

I remember how low and close we seemed to be flying to the

Interviewing President Paul Kagame

mountain between Bujumbura and Rwanda. As I looked out the window, the trees seemed so close that I felt like I could have touched them. It was beautiful and mildly terrifying all at once. I remember thinking, if whatever the man behind me has doesn't kill me, a crash sure will.

Needless to say, I survived. The crew didn't check on the man behind me once, but he survived the short flight too.

I was relieved to get off the flight to see the cleanest city I had ever visited. Kigali. I was gobsmacked by how clean it was.

Later, I met up with some people I had befriended on Twitter and they showed me around. Everyone spoke about the 2020 vision, which was to be the Singapore of Africa. Every single citizen told me about it. When I looked at the construction, the scaffolding that was everywhere, I could see the Singapore of Africa taking shape.

Every person I spoke to had a careful manner, as if they did not want to say the wrong thing. If I talked about Tutsis and Hutus, I was quickly told that there were no Hutu and Tutsis, just Rwandans. There was a tension I couldn't really put my finger on. In many ways, I could understand – it was a country that had gone through the most traumatic period just 17 years prior.

The following day, I was to interview President Paul Kagame at the presidential residence. I was picked up at the agreed time and on the way, noticed something I hadn't seen since apartheid South Africa: the military was patrolling the city with big guns. It was jarring and a shock to the system, taking me back to a bad time in South Africa.

When I arrived at the presidential compound, lunch had been prepared. Some of the people I had been with the day before were also there. We ate and chatted. The people surrounding the president were young and I found this satisfying. Each person I spoke to worked for the president in some capacity. I longed for the same for South Africa. No wonder Rwanda was changing at such a rapid rate. Kagame had surrounded himself with daring young people who were looking to create a future.

After lunch, I was ushered to the room where the interview would be conducted. The lighting had been set up. I was told that the president would be arriving soon. People started to straighten themselves. I couldn't tell whether what I was sensing was reverence, fear, respect, or all of these. There was something in the air.

When he walked in, there was absolute silence and his staff all stood with almost military precision even though none of them, I was sure, had been in the army.

This tall, lanky man who'd entered the room seemed almost too gentle to be commanding the kind of mixed emotions I was sensing. He was brought over to me and he shook my hand. I was casual but respectful. He was soft-spoken – something I did not expect. I had always been under the impression that in order for one to command the kind of adoration I'd picked up on from everyone I'd spoken to here, one needed to be extroverted and imposing. Paul Kagame was more charismatic than commanding.

His staff had told me not to ask him certain questions, specifically about running for another term or changing the constitution. I told them that I was here to ask questions that had been sent by YouTube viewers and that if some of those questions included these topics, too bad. I thought about the soldiers I had seen outside, the fact that I was in a foreign country, the fact that I was not even a journalist. I was a nobody in the bigger scheme of things. Would anyone notice if I vanished in Rwanda?

We made small talk for about 10 minutes. He wanted to know if I had been treated well. In the middle of our chat, I asked him if there were any questions that were out of bounds. He said there were none – I could ask him whatever I wanted. He needed to put the Rwandan story out there. I was relieved, and side-eyed the staff.

Eventually, we sat down, sitting directly opposite each other and facing each other. There was nothing between us.

I got my countdown from the camera crew. I had been practising this moment for ages because I did not want to screw up on camera. 'Hi, my name is Khaya Dlanga and I am here to interview President Paul Kagame of Rwanda for YouTube World View.' I had practised my opening line many times.

The lights were turned on. I turned to my right and looked into the camera. 'Hi, my name is Khaya Dlanga and I am here to interview President Paul Kagame of Nigeria—'

I heard a collective intake of air from all his staff. I was sure one staff member's eyes popped out. Their reaction gave me the distinct impression that I was about to be taken outside the presidential compound to be shot by the soldiers I had seen outside.

I broke into boisterous laughter and said, 'My apologies, Mr President. I have no idea what happened there!'

He laughed with me, a hearty laugh – hearty by his reticent standards anyway – and his staff finally exhaled.

Sometimes an innocent thing may not come across as innocent

It was the year of our Lord Jesus Christ of Nazareth and everywhere else, 2012, and I was having a book launch with several other authors who were part of a series of books called The Youngsters. Our publisher had the great idea of launching all the books at the same time in the hope of getting young people to buy all the books. Back then, I was a bit younger and even better looking, if you can believe that's even humanly possible.

The Youngsters writers were Anele Mdoda, who, if you don't mind me bragging, is a very good friend of mine; Shaka Sisulu, another friend of mine; Danny K and Nick Rabinowitz, whom I had met many years ago in Cape Town when I was a thriving but minor comedian in the city of the colonisers. (*Nods to *Black Panther**)

On the morning of the launch, I woke up earlier than usual because Sophie, who has the thankless task of cleaning for me, washing my dishes, and ironing my clothes, was going to be arriving at my place.

As the diligent person she is, she would often leave me a love note: please buy washing power, Toilet Duck, Mr Min, tile cleaner, Handy Andy, and so on and so forth and stuff like that. I had foolishly forgotten to buy the goods she had instructed me to get the week before.

After showering, I received a phone call from a beautiful lady who lived in my complex.

'Hi, Khaya,' she said.

'Who wants me?' I said.

She laughed. 'No, man, do you have water?' she asked.

'I do.'

'I don't know what's wrong. I have no water. Can I come to your place to shower?' she asked.

I had known her for years and we had a lot of friends in common. I knew all her beautiful friends because beautiful people must be known.

But my mind started racing. What will I be doing while she is showering in my small apartment? What must I do with myself in the meantime? Isn't it going to be awkward? Will I make her feel uncomfortable? Will she arrive wrapped in a towel?

'All right,' I said in a calm, unfazed voice. Like this is the sort of thing that happens every day. Hot women wanting to use my shower. 'Listen, I need to go get stuff for my helper. I am about to leave to get stuff from the Woolies at the Engen because the other shops aren't open yet. I will leave my door unlocked for you, and will leave the key so that you can lock it while you're showering. I'll probably be out of here in about five minutes.'

I was already dressed and just needed to brush my teeth. When I was done, I went to my car and drove to the garage, which was less than two kilometres away.

I took my precious time just buying the products Sophie had so lovingly requested in her note. Then I filled up with petrol. Took my time with that too.

After about 20 minutes, I drove back to my place, hoping that she would not be there. I drove slow, like Kanye West says in his song, 'Drive slow, homie.' I even parked slowly. Walked slowly to the apartment too.

As I approached, I sharpened my ears so that I could hear if the shower was still on. To my relief, it wasn't. I listened for movement in the apartment. None. I knocked and waited. I knocked again. I called out her name. This was just in case I walked in and she was … well, in the fashion of Eve in the Garden of Eden. Still, there was silence.

I opened the door, hoping she wasn't there. She wasn't. Relief. I fetched my work bag, locked up and went to work. Uneventful, you say. Well, just wait for the next instalment.

Before going to the book launch I asked a friend of mine, Sindi Ndlovu, to pick up my then girlfriend, Priscilla Menoe, from my apartment. They would be going to the launch together.

I arrived for the book launch at Sandton City, where I had to go to a coffee shop to sign copies of my book. I left a different and personalised message in each book.

We were then ushered to the open area and we all took our places. Mandy Wiener, who was also the editor of all the books in the series, was also going to interview all of us on stage.

While I was up there, my heart skipped a few beats. I was no longer nervous about the book launch. I was nervous about what I suddenly noticed from where I was sitting. I saw Sindi and Priscilla, together with the beautiful lady who had showered at my place that morning. Even though I had done nothing wrong, I panicked. They seemed relaxed at least.

The panel discussion came to an end and I looked at my phone as we stepped down from the stage. There was a message from my neighbour: 'Oh my God, Khaya. I was walking with Sindi and Priscilla and I was telling Sindi how I had no water and had to shower at your place. I had no idea Priscilla was your girlfriend. All I could see was Sindi's face trying to tell me to stop. I am so sorry!' She thought she had ruined my relationship.

I knew there and then that it would look like there was something more to the story because I hadn't told Priscilla about it. People were congratulating me on my book and I was shaking their hands but I was worried that I was about to be dumped on the day of my book launch. Still, I was calm, shaking hands like a politician running for office.

I eventually made my way to the trio, Sindi, Priscilla and the lady who'd showered at my place earlier. I hugged them hello, then I looked at Priscilla while gesturing towards my neighbour. 'I see you met the person who showered at my place this morning.' I saw relief in their eyes.

'She told us!' Priscilla and Sindi said at the same time. We all laughed about it.

Later that evening, on my way home with Priscilla, she straight up told me that had I never said anything, she would have said congratulations on my book, then vanished into the crowd and I would have never seen her again.

It was on that day I realised that a perfectly innocent event can look very different to outsiders.

Lunch with Xolisa and William Shatner (aka Denny Crane)

One random Saturday, my cousin Xolisa Dyeshana called me to say he was about to have lunch with William Shatner, who was in South Africa to shoot an advert for an insurance company. Xolisa was a creative director on the job and he is an easily likeable person, so I can see why Denny Crane would have wanted to spend more time with him after the shoot.

Xolisa was supposed to have had dinner with William Shatner and the rest of the production team two nights before, but being the dedicated cousin he is, he had skipped the dinner to go to the launch of my first book.

William Shatner, in his infinite kindness, decided that he would still have lunch with Xolisa the day he was meant to leave to go back to the States.

My cousin knew that I was a big *Boston Legal* fan – I had all the DVDs of the television series. We were both fans, and we especially loved the scenes at the end of every episode where Denny Crane, played by William Shatner, and Alan Shore, played by James Spader, would sit on the balcony and wax philosophical while drinking whiskey and smoking cigars.

I do not even remember what I was doing at the Rosebank Mall when Xolisa called me because everything before that phone call seems meaningless.

'Chap,' Xolisa said on the other end of the line. (For those who who haven't realised by now, 'chap' has somehow managed to become Xhosa lingo. I remember reading *Long Walk to Freedom* and noticing how often Mandela used the word in his book. It occurred to me that Xhosa folks completely appropriated 'chap' long ago.) 'Drop whatever you're doing and come meet me at the Saxon.'

'Why?' I asked.

'I am about to meet William Shatner for lunch.'

I ran to an Exclusive Books immediately and went to buy the newly published *In My Arrogant Opinion*. I was extremely embarrassed because it was the first time I'd bought my own book. My face was slam-bam on the cover. It was impossible to hide. The cashier looked at the book, then back at me.

'Is this you?' she asked.

'Yes,' I said.

'How does it feel to have your face on the cover of a book?'

'Narcissistic,' I replied.

She laughed and gave me back the book. I asked her to lend me a pen so I could write an inscription for William Shatner.

I then drove like the wind from Rosebank to the Saxon Hotel in Sandhurst, about five kilometres away. All within the legal speed limit, of course. After parking my car and being driven to the entrance of the prestigious establishment, I walked calmly for about two seconds before sprinting like a man possessed. Why the security did not tackle me is still a mystery to this day.

I saw them sitting outside. Mr *Star Trek* Captain. Mr *Rescue 911*. Mr Denny Crane. The one-and-only William Shatner, with my cousin.

I approached them slowly, trying to make sure that I didn't look overly eager. Xolisa stood up and said, 'That's my cousin, Khaya.'

'Aah, the one with the book launch the other day?' he asked.

'Yes,' Xolisa replied.

'Hi, Mr Shatner,' I said as I shook his hand.

I reached into the Exclusive Books packet, pulled out my book and said, 'And here it is.'

'*In My Arrogant Opinion* by Khaya Dlanga. Is that how you say your name?' he said as he extended the book away from him like old people do when they have forgotten their glasses.

'You want me to sign it?' he asked me.

'No, I signed it for you.'

At this, he laughed so hard. It was the last thing he'd expected. He wiped a little tear from his eye.

'You spend your life signing things for people. I figured I should give you a rest – that's why I signed this for you.' I opened the book to where I had written him a message.

'I'm going to read it tonight on my way back home. Thank you so much.'

We sat down and engaged in conversation about everything: South Africa, its place in the world, religion, and his daughter who was extremely religious. He wanted to know our views on religion. He seemed troubled by his daughter's unquestioning adoption of

Christianity. I told him that I was a Christian but I do not follow my preacher's words as gospel, nor do I not question the faith.

He seemed to have a genuine interest in people and to be an amazing listener. When William Shatner listens to you, it is like he is listening with his whole body. He had razor focus on what I was saying to him, as if the only thing that mattered were the words coming out of my mouth. His eyes did not leave me when I was speaking.

At one point, he called a waiter over and said, 'Get me three of your most expensive cigars and whiskies,' which he followed up with, 'Actually, if this was your place and money was not an issue, which cigar would you give me? Get me those cigars.'

Xolisa and I smiled. We were about to be treated.

When I'd arrived, I was worried that we had no more than 30 minutes, but our great conversation lasted almost three hours.

Eventually, William Shatner had to go back to his hotel room to meet his wife, pack his bags and leave for the airport. He stood up, shook our hands and thanked us for being interesting. Then he said, 'All right, you fellows are paying,' and left.

Xolisa and I looked at each other. Payday was a week away; we were still low-level employees then and this ninja had ordered some of the best whiskey and three of the most expensive cigars – at the Saxon.

I could see the panic in Xolisa's eyes. Were his eyes watering? Maybe my eyes were watering. There was a moment of silence, as we probably thought the same thing: *How much was each cigar?*

We asked for the bill, but when it arrived, neither of us wanted to open it, the words, 'Most expensive cigars and whiskies,' ringing in our ears. After losing a game of Rock-Paper-Scissors, I opened it and forced myself to look at the total. Luckily, we had just enough money between the two of us to pay for the bill. We didn't know how we would survive the rest of the month.

Cigars: Exorbitant.

Whiskies: Daylight robbery.

Three hours with William Shatner: Priceless.

Keeping my composure around Cassper

The most awkward thing happened one day. I have a horrible habit: if someone says something, I will use what they said and turn it into a tune (terribly, of course). For example, if someone says, 'Will you be there?' I will start singing to the Michael Jackson tune, 'Will you be thereeeeeheee.'

We were shooting a prank video for Amstel South Africa. As marketing manager on the brand, I had to be there to supervise the shoot and make decisions.

A huge Cassper Nyovest fan was going to come to a restaurant with his sister, who was in on the prank. The sister would encourage him to pick a song on the jukebox, knowing he would definitely choose Cassper's song. Once he selected the song, the jukebox would open up, smoke coming out of it, and boom, the real Cassper would walk out, mic in hand.

Back in the control room, where we were watching the rehearsals before our prankee and his sister arrived, one of my colleagues, Dimakatso Napiane, said, 'I hope that waitress maintains her composure when she sees Cassper.'

It was at that point that I started singing, 'Composure, compos—'

I suddenly realised what I had done. Cassper was right next to me. This was right in the middle of the alleged feud between AKA and Cassper.

There was a brief silence but Cassper laughed his ass off. Boy, was I embarrassed.

I believe the children are the future

December in East London is a beautiful blur. The sun is out and bright, and there are bouts of humidity. The people are as happy as the sun. Many of us who live in big cities like Johannesburg, Durban and Cape Town make our Great Trek back home from the 15th of December for what has been termed 'Big Dayz' (that being December holidays).

Happiness overflows. Everyone is kind and generous. Those of us from Johannesburg notice the familiar sounds of Xhosa everywhere once again. People who have driven from Johannesburg have also stopped at a Shell garage to fill up and buy a delicious Shamrock Pie. The bite welcomes you to the Eastern Cape on your way to East London. People swear by it. In December, many of these pies are eaten in the middle of night and early mornings, in garages everywhere. As holiday-makers descend on the area, the pies vanish quicker.

It was during one of these December holidays that I flew down to East London Airport to be picked up by my cousin, Xolisa Dyeshana, my ever-present accomplice.

He was already waiting outside when I got there. The airport had not yet been renovated and you could park just outside arrivals. He had arrived in the city a few days before and his mood was *holiday*. He wore a T-shirt, shades and flip-flops. It was overcast but humid. Optimism, perhaps even a bit of carefree mischievousness, filled the air.

We greeted each other, and put my bags in the boot of his car. As we closed the boot, a big car parked behind Xolisa's car. As we were about to drive off, the car behind us hooted, and out stepped a great friend of ours, who was also my neighbour in Johannesburg.

Much excitement ensued. She was at the airport to pick up her sister who was landing in the next 15 minutes, so we decided to wait with her.

I started with a game Xolisa and I used to play, saying, 'You know, Xolisa, I believe the children are the future. We should teach them and let them lead the way.'

'Show them all the beauty they possess inside,' Xolisa said with fervour.

'Yes, give them a sense of pride,' I responded.

'To make it easier,' Xolisa replied, uninterrupted.

Our friend was standing there silently, listening intently to what we were saying.

'And you know what?' I said.

'What?' Xolisa asked.

'Let the children's laughter remind us of how we used to be.'

Our friend suddenly turned to look and us and said with great passion, 'It's easy for you guys to say. For example, if you look at how we grew up, it wasn't that simple.'

Xolisa and I looked at each other, holding back laughter. I could not keep it in and I burst out laughing so loud that the people in the airport turned to look.

'Why are you guys laughing? I am serious,' she said, disheartened.

I was literally on the airport floor; Xolisa was laughing uncontrollably and she was still staring at us in confusion. Perhaps she wondered if we had smoked something of the green variety.

I was laughing too hard to explain.

My thoughts on relationships

1. A relationship should mean freedom, not control.
2. There is no need to police each other. Nobody owns anybody. Even your parents don't own you.
3. Don't force or stay in a relationship because you are lonely.
4. If compromise is excessive and one-sided, that's rarely a recipe for a great relationship.
5. Stop believing in the delusion that a conflict-filled relationship is passionate. It isn't.
6. If they make you feel like being in a relationship with you is a favour, leave.
7. Everyone has a past. When getting into a new relationship, the state of your current character should matter more than your past.
8. Don't allow yourself to be guilted into staying in a relationship you don't want to be in.
9. When you fight, don't focus on winning the argument at the cost of finding a solution.
10. Be in a healthy and loving relationship with yourself first.
11. Don't force permanence into a temporary situation. Sometimes people are meant to be in our lives for a season. And that's okay.

12. If you are constantly walking on eggshells in a relationship, it's time to re-evaluate your relationship.

Lyrical thesis

The art of kwaito is lost on a lot of people.

Music can move people, or simply confound them because they have absolutely no idea what the musician is trying to say (leaving those of us who can't dance thinking about the lyrics, instead of dancing to the groove).

I am about to expose you to my analysis of some of the most popular kwaito songs over the past two decades.

Such a thesis must mention the legendary Thembi Seete from Boom Shaka.

When we were younger, we marvelled at her rhyming skills and repeated what she said. We did not know what she meant, because we couldn't speak English back then and some would say, later on, that neither could she. But they could not be further from the truth. Allow me.

Many people incorrectly concluded that the line 'I don't know what can I do with myself' was a case of Seete's bad English. It wasn't. It was a case of unrecognised genius by 'the masses of our people', to borrow a phrase from Thabo Mbeki, 'and so on and so forth and stuff like that', to borrow another. 'I don't know what can I do with myself' is a clear demonstration of excitement. She is so excited that her ability 'to can', so to speak, is uncontainable, uncontrollable, and demands to be expressed.

When one is immensely excited, one's sense of language and the ability to put words together in a coherent manner are greatly diminished (it is not unlike when you, as a black person, are really angry and all the English your parents paid good money for flies out the window). She cleverly indicated her overwhelming sense of excitement not just by saying that she did not know what to do with herself, but by being excited to the point of incoherence. She did not just say it – she became it. Pure genius. But your minds were not big enough to recognise this genius, you mere mortals. You were never ready. In fact, you are still not ready.

Second up, is the legendary, pint-sized star, Msawawa – a man whose age has remained a mystery for years.

'Yes! Yes! Yes! Yes! Yes!' he sings in 'Bowungakanani'. In the first 'yes', Msawawa is exclaiming that it is indeed him in the music video featuring a young child. In the second one, he is emphasising that it is indeed him, like he said earlier with some patience. In the third, he is absolutely certain and affirms his first three yesses.

The final two mark his extreme irritation. He rapidly repeats these to ensure that the doubters are silenced by his proclamations.

The grandness that is Msawawa himself is so awesome and so huge that even he can only refer to himself in the third person. This is evidenced by the phrase 'ngu Msawawa lo!' ('This is Msawawa!').

For him to say, 'I am Msawawa' would have caused many unnecessary deaths in a nuclear explosion that could have exterminated half the world, yet only half of Msawawa. His awesomeness is so awesome that even he cannot say it. This is the reason he sings, 'Ngizohleka one hour' ('I will laugh for one hour') because even he cannot explain his own awesomeness. Attempting to explain himself is laughable.

Finally, we have Unathi, who wanted to know from Zola who Noxolo was ('Ngubani uNoxolo?'). This was a pertinent question. Zola simply said he had no idea. Zola also said, 'She's just a friend,' yet he didn't have her number or home address. What sort of friend was this? We also wanted to know.

Yes, 'just a friend' yet he does not have her address? 'Thyini, le chap!' ('Wow, this guy!') we exclaimed and clapped once.

How on earth is it possible? Does he take her for a fool? I asked myself all these questions. We all wanted to know this Noxolo. But the more I thought about it, the more I understood what Zola was on about.

We actually all know Noxolo. She friend-zoned the whole of South Africa for years. And we all thought she was a friend but she didn't know who we are. We don't have her number or her address. All we knew was what time we would see her: 7:30 pm. Her friend-zoning game was deep. She friend-zoned us every night. It is the one-and-only 'Ndini thanda nonke, 'makhaya' ('I love you all at home') Noxolo Grootboom.

Zola was not lying. He just didn't realise he was friend-zoned. I hope I have been able to answer who Noxolo is for you, Unathi.

Men holding hands

I remember seeing a photograph of former President Nelson Mandela walking hand in hand with Zimbabwe's President Robert Mugabe. There is also one of Mandela walking hand in hand with Archbishop Emeritus Desmond Tutu and another of Mugabe holding hands with former President Thabo Mbeki.

In December 2013, at Mandela's funeral, as I walked through his home towards the marquee, I noticed two elderly Xhosa men walking hand in hand; the scene reminded me of my childhood, growing up in the then Transkei in the Eastern Cape. Hand-holding was a common, everyday thing. You still see older people do it in villages, but we have lost this practice now in the suburbs and townships.

Old people would hold your hand while talking to you, especially if they hadn't seen you for a long time. They would hold it for a while, long after the greeting, often an indication of how much they liked and missed you. Your hand would be moved from palm to palm as you two spoke. The smile in their faces would be visible in their eyes too.

'Kunjani eGoli? Awunqabe. Awusemhle. Uzeka nini? Unayo imoto? Usa yihamba inkonzo? Kutheni ngathi awutyi eGoli wabhitya kangaka? Ufana noyihlo.' ('How is Johannesburg? You're scarce. You're so good looking. When are you getting married? Do you have a car? Do you still go to church? Why are you so skinny – are you not eating in Johannesburg? You look just like your father.') They could have a conversation with you for 10 minutes while your hand was in theirs.

Maybe it was because they knew that young people were always in a hurry and they wanted to connect with us.

Walking around while holding someone else's hand was not just something that men did. Women also walked hand in hand, at times clinging to each other. They would stop, slapping each other's hands as they laughed and talked.

The hand-holding was a demonstration of closeness, friendship and trust. It was a symbol of openness and full acceptance of the other person, simply for their humanity. It symbolised so many things that cannot be put into words. It was so natural that we were never even aware that we were doing it. It was as natural as pulling WWE moves on your younger brother.

Of course, there is nothing wrong with getting rid of customs that don't serve us – culture is ever evolving. But it is shocking how easily we black South Africans have run away from our traditions and assimilated Western culture. And there is really no one to blame but ourselves: we have allowed ourselves to be convinced that what is Western is better. There is nothing wrong with African culture – but there is everything wrong with us if we think there is.

When formerly whites-only schools were opened to black pupils, I was one of the first black children to attend Hudson Park Primary School in East London.

Two men holding hands at Mandela's funeral in Qunu, Eastern Cape

As black children, we'd often walk around holding hands because it was something we had seen older people do. It was the surest sign of friendship. It was normal and everyone did it.

When I went to Hudson Park Primary, black boys and girls often held hands when they walked together. White children would walk past and say: 'Why are you guys holding hands? You guys are gay.'

And I'd say yes, because to me, 'gay' meant only one thing. At Little Flower Junior Secondary School, we'd read a short story in which the word 'gay' was described as 'cheerful, happy and jolly'. I still remember the story speaking about a 'gay meadow' (I had also looked up the word 'meadow'). The more the white children said, 'All the black guys are gay,' the more I realised that their tone was negative.

I looked the word up again and I found another meaning for that word. I knew very little then about the LGBTQ community, and all I had ever heard was negative. Later, it was largely due to self-education and my love of reading that I rejected the idea of labelling different sexual orientations as 'other'.

At the time, we black children stopped walking hand in hand. In our quest for acceptance into a new world, we had just allowed other people to tell us how we should behave and what we should believe.

When my friend paid R50k to have lunch with me

My friends Ciko Thomas, Kholisa Thomas and Nomkhita Nqweni are on the board of a not-for-profit organisation called Ubuntu Pathways, which does some great work for township communities in Port Elizabeth.

Using funds raised by the organisation, Ubuntu has built a centre where nurses, doctors and social workers help take care of community members. It has been built in the middle of a township and has won international architectural awards. I have been there and it is a wonder.

Ubuntu's philosophy is raising children from cradle to career. The clinic takes care of the needs of the community, and HIV-positive pregnant women can receive regular check-ups. So far, they have 100 per cent success rate in delivering babies who are HIV negative. The centre offers children after-school care, where they also get food. After matric, these students are assisted with the adjustment to tertiary education.

I have now been co-opted by Ciko, Kholisa and Nomkhita to be part of the host committee for the annual fundraising gala dinner. But before that, in 2016, I was just an attendant at the glitzy first annual South African Ubuntu Gala Dinner.

Through this gala dinner, funds are raised by way of donations from corporates, purchasing of tables, and auctioning off various items. (Nelson Makamo's works of art have been popular over the past few years.)

In that first year, I too was to be auctioned off: 'Lunch with the Author of *To Quote Myself*' was the offering. I was incredibly self-conscious – mostly due to the fear of being auctioned off for no more than R300.

When my name was called up by the auctioneer as the final item on the bill, I felt a sudden hot flush all over my short frame. I waved as I was introduced and there was polite applause. A Nelson Makamo artwork had just been auctioned off for over R100 000. I was the last item and people had already spent their money. I figured they were too broke now. Besides, even I wouldn't want to have lunch with me – why would anyone else?

After waving to everyone, I went to sit next to another friend of mine, Litha Nkombisa. The auction began at R1 000. I was already relieved because it started off at more than the R300 I was dreading. I had already overachieved.

It quickly went up to R3 000, then R10 000. Who on earth would want to have lunch with me so much? I was more than happy. There were two tables who were bidding against each other. The figure quickly went past R16 000, and kept going up until it got to R30 000.

It looked like the R30 000 table was going to win the bid. I heard Litha say, 'Who are these woman who want to have lunch with my friend? We don't know those people.'

Litha raised his hand and shouted, 'Soze, yichap yethu le, he can't be having lunch with women we don't know!' He stood up and said, 'R50 000!'

There was much laughter and the auctioneer asked for R51 000. There were no more bids and I was sold to Litha for lunch. Hilariously, I always have dinner or lunch with him and my other friends at least once a week anyway.

His rationale was that he was saving me from strangers – who knew what they were going to do to me.

How to take a break from being worked to death at home

For most black people in South Africa, I imagine, going back home for a traditional ceremony, a funeral, a wedding or even Christmas, means there is a lot of work that needs to be done – be it cutting a slaughtered sheep or cow to pieces, or roasting meat, or working your butt off in the kitchen. At some point, you just want a break. You need to be at peace, at one with laziness. But old people don't like to see someone doing nothing when they can see there is still a lot to be done.

There is also always something someone forgot to buy in town. If you have a driver's licence and a car, you will have to drive around to buy whatever is needed. If you have a job, well, you will have to pay for whatever is needed. These are unwritten, unspoken rules. Everybody knows what their role is in these great family productions.

One of the greatest tricks you can deploy in order to avoid this thankless work is very simple – an age-old trick. It's been tried and tested. By me. It works.

Since our families are so big, there is always some cousin or relative who has a baby. Without fail.

If you need a break, simply grab a baby, preferably not one who cries a lot and needs to have his mother around all the time. That will be trouble.

The relative is often always so relieved that someone else is looking after their child that they will give up the baby easily. It is important, though, that you are naturally good with kids. Luckily, I am.

Once the baby is your arms, make sure that everyone can see that you have the child in your arms, and that you are either feeding him or putting him to sleep or trying to stop him from crying.

Nobody wants to disturb someone with a baby. Everybody else will be sent to do everything else, but the person holding the baby will always be exempt from the work.

Trust me, it works.

A man offers a woman a job, then hits on her

Many men will say, 'I am not like Harvey Weinstein.' But how many men promise women opportunities, wine and dine them, buy them gifts, and then expect some kind of transactional relationship to follow? Men must stop abusing their power.

Guys, this is why women say we are trash. Many men will act as though they are helping a woman, but they're only dangling their promises in front of her to exert power over her.

Coercion is not consent. If, for example, you promise her a job and she agrees to have sex with you, it is coercion. There is no real free will. Often, people are desperate. It is the women who are shamed for securing jobs or 'favours' in this way – but the men who put them in these positions aren't. That has got to change.

As recently as September 2017, a close friend of mine told me a story that made me feel angry and powerless. I couldn't do anything about it. If I felt so powerless, I could not imagine how much more powerless she must have felt.

My friend had met a gentleman who owns a successful company. He knew that she needed a job and he'd recommended her for an open position at his company. The whole process was handled professionally, through his HR department. The interview had gone very well; the HP practitioner was very impressed; and the owner of the company had not been visibly involved. My friend felt hopeful and confident. She had no reason to be apprehensive about the process or the position because the man had shown no signs of being, for lack of a better word, trash.

A few days after the interview, she received a text from the owner of the company. He said that he'd heard that the interview went very well; he used words like 'babe' and 'sweetie'. Her heart sank and she immediately felt uncomfortable. She knew that this was not headed in the right direction. She did not respond to his text.

He then called and left her a voicemail, saying they should go celebrate with a drink that night because the job was hers.

There was a part of her that wanted to use the easy excuse of having other plans. Instead, she decided to be direct. She politely declined the drinks invite as she viewed it as unprofessional, explaining that she didn't want to create the wrong impression.

The next day she got a phone call from HR, telling her that unfortunately, she did not get the job. The night before, the owner had wanted to celebrate with her and when she did not respond to his advances, the offer was rescinded.

There are many more stories like this – not only of opportunities that qualified women don't get when they stand up for themselves, but also of harassment in the workplace on a day-to-day basis. Many women don't feel that they would be protected if they speak up. If anything, they are often victimised more. Our social structure protects men.

We not only need systems that make it easier for women to report this kind of behaviour, but clear and actionable consequences for perpetrators.

What my friend told me bothered me for months. We are not entitled to women.

Act my personality, not my age

Someone asked me a very interesting question on Twitter: 'What's your secret to always being happy?' The first thing I thought was: 'Am I actually always happy?' The truth is I am happy. A lot. Sometimes it feels like we are not supposed to say or show how happy we are.

I think happiness has a lot to do with actively getting rid of negative energies, so my answer to this question was: I don't hold grudges. If you hold grudges, you are actively participating in your own unhappiness.

I don't spend time thinking about what could have been. It's gone – no use thinking about it.

I don't dislike others. It's negative.

I do not control others. If you try to control someone else, there must be something profoundly unhappy in you. I give people freedom to be themselves because I also want them to be comfortable with me being me.

I don't take myself too seriously. People who take themselves too seriously spend too much time telling themselves what they are not supposed to do. They are more concerned about appearances than the satisfaction of their soul. I try as much as I can not to deny my soul.

I don't spend too much time wondering what people think about me. I am perfectly happy being silly and living a childlike existence. This is why I think it's important to act your personality because it is a link to your soul.

When my tyre burst in a dark, dingy place

One night, while travelling back from an event in Johannesburg, I hit a pothole. I was driving a Mercedes-Benz C-Class, it was late at night, and I was in a dangerous area, near the CBD.

At first, I thought the tyre was fine, so I drove on for a few minutes. Then I felt the car veer to the right. Soon, the tyre carcass was slapping the car and I could hear loud bangs with each rotation of the wheel. It felt like the carcass was damaging my car but I was too fearful to stop in this dark and dingy area. I had suddenly become one of those people who imagines every horror story they have heard about being hijacked, robbed and attacked.

I soldiered on, driving slowly. There was a garage some 600 metres away. If I could just drive a little bit further, I told myself, I could make it there.

The car began to feel like it was lifting and landing on the front right wheel, and I soon realised I had to stop. There was nothing more I could do. I could see the garage – so close but so far.

I got out to begin changing the tyre and I won't lie – my mouth was in my throat the whole time.

I opened the boot very quickly and looked around to make sure there was no one there to surprise me with a sudden attack. I then opened the flap on the floor of the boot and quickly took out the spare wheel and all the equipment required to change a tyre. The spare was a proper tyre – not one of those biscuit ones – so it was heavy. In my mind, I was trying not to appear scared while doing this, but I am pretty sure I looked like the most nervous man in all of Westeros.

Maybe some two or three years before this, I had just learnt to drive and had bought my first car. While driving from Johannesburg to what was then a new Valpré water plant in Heidelberg, I hit a pothole on a narrow road. The tyre deflated as fast as a pricked balloon.

I was in the middle of nowhere and had never changed a tyre. Yes, I was that person who didn't know how to change a tyre. However, if you wanted to slaughter a sheep or milk a cow, I was your guy.

I called Mercedes for help, and they told it would take them about two hours to get to me. I tried AA, but it would also take them a while.

I had a genius idea – let me ask Twitter: 'How do I change a tyre?' I was asked for a picture of the tyre, the car and equipment, and then given a step-by-step tutorial by those great internet people. An hour later, I was on my merry way.

That year, I would have to change 14 tyres after incidents with potholes. It was embarrassing.

Now, after hitting another pothole, in the middle of the night in a scary area, the first thing I reached for in the boot was a spanner – to use as a weapon if I needed one. A group of guys walked past and I just stood there with my spanner and tried to look unbothered. They asked me if I needed help but I was very suspicious of them, so I told them AA was five minutes away and they left. My overactive imagination had my heart racing.

Then an old man in an old Cressida stopped and asked if I needed help. I felt bad and told him I was okay. He drove off.

After all my practice over the past few years, I could change tyres really fast. But here, it was too dark to see what I was doing. I was also too scared to spend too much time bending over, in case I got attacked. I must have been as scared as all the other motorists who didn't stop because they were probably suspicious about whether I really needed help or whether I was just some guy trying to rob them.

I realised after the Cressida drove off that I needed help with lighting. Cars kept driving past and no one stopped, even when I tried to flag them down. After some time, another old man stopped. This one was in his sixties, from the Eastern Cape, and driving a beaten-up early-80s Mercedes-Benz.

He parked his car behind mine then got out his car and started changing the tyre. I told him I could do it but he insisted. He said he wanted to help – he didn't just want to stand there. Besides, if tsotsis came, he said, I was young and strong enough to fight them off while he changed the tyre. He laughed.

I stood there feeling awkward and guilty while this old man changed my tyre. When he was done, he went to his car to fetch a bottle of water for us to clean our hands.

He told me he'd pulled over because he could see I needed help and he knew people never stop to help. I asked him to follow me to the next petrol station, where I filled his tank. At first he refused, saying he didn't stop because he wanted to get something from me. I told him that I also wanted to do this little bit for him, even though I knew he didn't do it to get something out of me. It was the least I could do.

Ubuntu still exists but it's becoming rarer. Lack of trust is the reason we don't help each other any more. May God bless that old man.

Instant reply

The curse of immediacy. Permanent, constant accessibility has given rise to the illusion of validity. If you send me a message and I answer you immediately, for some people, that somehow demonstrates how valid or important you are in my life. This is a false idea.

This is the reason I have no notifications whatsoever on my phone, except for phone calls. No WhatsApp, iMessage, social media or email notifications. I want to look at my phone when I want to look at it – not when it tells me to.

Also, the contest of who texts first plays into imaginary power games. If you want to text someone, text them. If they don't answer immediately, they are probably busy with other things; it doesn't mean they think any less of you. If they reject your advances, that is also okay.

Why is our value suddenly defined by who sends a text first or how quickly they respond or if they decide to respond at all?

Bosso ke mang?

One year, I was invited by Vodacom to the Durban July and as a person who likes nice, free things, I happily obliged.

I had heard many stories about the Durban July. I'd heard of some people suddenly having family funerals or emergencies in Durban during the weekend of the July because they didn't want their partners to come with. The event has gained a 'what happens in Vegas, stays in Vegas' quality about it. I was curious. I wanted to go watch the people rather than the horses. The horse race is the last thing people talk about.

I was to fly to Durban with my then girlfriend, Priscilla Menoe. We got to OR Tambo International Airport on time and presented our identity documents with confidence.

'Sir,' said the gentleman behind the counter, 'I'm sorry – you're not on this flight.'

'That's impossible. I am on the next flight to Durban,' I replied with the ego of a man who has a beautiful woman next to him and wants to appear like he has things under control. I turned to look at her and gave her a reassuring smile and nod.

'Sir,' the gentleman said in a low voice, as though not to embar-

The awkward photograph taken by Pako Lefifi at the Durban July

rass me in front of the lady, 'your ticket is for Lanseria Airport, not OR Tambo.'

'What?' I grabbed the ticket. There. In black and white, it said Lanseria. I was deflated. Like most people who were born inland and far, far away from the ocean, Priscilla had been looking forward to going to the Durban. She wanted to see the waves and the sea.

There was no way we could make it to Lanseria and catch the flight on time. I tried to find what time the next flight was and if we could get on it. The flights were fully booked. I was so embarrassed, not just for disappointing my girlfriend by not double-checking the tickets, but for missing my flight to Durban after my travel, accommodation and entertainment had been covered by Vodacom.

I started lying to myself and to Priscilla: 'I didn't wanna go anyway.'

'Yeah, me too.' She also lied, so we were even.

I went through my emails and called the lady who had been organising my flights. I told her, with a heavy heart, that I had rushed to the wrong airport and there was no way I would be able to make it. I apologised most sincerely. She told me not to worry, that she was going to see if she could make a plan. A few minutes later, my phone rang.

'Hi, Mr Dlanga, I managed to get you a flight to Durban.'

'What? What do you mean? They just told me that all the flights are fully booked.'

'Yes, but not business class. You will be flying business to Durban.'

'Really?'

'Yes, really. Check your email. We have already sent the details and arranged for you to be picked up from the airport in Durban.' Just like that, I got my very first (and only) domestic business-class ticket.

I hung up and told Priscilla that we were going to Durban after all. 'And we're flying business!' Our recent lies to each other about not wanting to go to Durban were quickly forgotten.

We enjoyed the flight – all two minutes of it because it's so close: you blink once and you're already there.

We arrived. Had dinner. Mingled. Went to bed.

The following day was event day. We woke up and had breakfast. When we were getting dressed, Priscilla suddenly realised that she had forgotten her shoes in Joburg. I couldn't believe it. I was the annoyed yet understanding, and impatient but patient boyfriend. Yes, it's possible to be all these things when you are a boyfriend. You're irritated because now you suddenly have less time and have to rush to find a mall in a city you do not know. On the other hand, you also know that you can't be visibly annoyed because she is already frustrated and doesn't even know if she will find the kind of shoe that will go with the dress she wants to wear.

We went to some small mall, not too far away, and found a pair of shoes she could somewhat live with. Boy, did they pinch her feet. I looked at her and said, 'I'm telling you those are too high and you'll complain about how painful they are within 30 minutes of wearing them,' but, Miss These Are Very Comfortable And I Will Be Fine decided to buy them anyway.

At the Durban July, we saw horses at some point but we never watched the races. We moved between the various marquees, having a good time. We were invited to one where there was going to be a live band, and the marquee was packed – except for a couch right in front, where there was just enough space for two people.

I froze. I looked at the two empty spaces. Priscilla also froze.

The reason we both stood there, not knowing what to do, was because the two empty seats were next to Boity Thulo. She had been my girlfriend before I started dating Priscilla.

Boity looked at where we were standing and waved to us. I hesitated. Priscilla did not think twice – she approached the couch. I think her shoes made the decision for her at that point. She had been complaining about how painful they were.

Once we got to the couch, I realised that if I sat down as we were, I would be sitting in between the two of them. What to do? Do I sit next to Boity and be in between my previous girlfriend and my current? I stood there like a deer in headlights, my back to the stage and looking at this situation, which ranked as one of the most awkward.

Priscilla moved past me, shook Boity's hand and sat in between myself and Boity. I didn't know whether to feel relieved or nervous. Could this be any more awkward?

At some point, I heard someone shout, 'Khaya!' I looked up. Blam. Something flashed in my eye. It was a photographer. I knew exactly what had happened. The photographer had noticed that I was with my ex and my new girlfriend.

I brushed it off.

Fast-forward to the Monday after the Durban July. I was at the office in meetings all morning. At 1:30 pm, I looked at my phone. I had a high number of mentions on social media. It was strange because I hadn't tweeted a thing that day. I panicked. What did I do? I opened the Twitter app.

It was the photo. Comments were raging from, 'How awkward!' to 'Bosso ke mang?' ('Who is the boss?') Of course, there was much laughter on the feed. It had appeared on the tabloid website, Just Curious, with the headline, 'Bosso Ke Mang?' and a caption below the photo: 'Khaya Dlanga with his girlfriend and ex'. That was it. Nothing else. As if they had no names of their own. I could see the humour in it. I laughed out loud when I saw it. It was hilarious. Awkward as hell. No wonder Twitter was having a field day with it.

Let me attempt to describe the situation. The couch had enough space for three people. Boity was reclining away from Priscilla, looking in the opposite direction. Priscilla's knees were slightly turned towards me and she was looking at the band.

Now to me. My eyes looked like I had just been caught stealing

R5 from my mother's purse. I was looking directly into the camera, with my drink dangling between my legs. When the photo was taken, I said to myself, 'This is not going to be good.'

The photo was awkward and there was no denying it.

What the photo did not show was the long conversation the two of them had had. The reason the body language seemed so uncomfortable was because Boity had been called to chat to a person who was on the couch next to her. Priscilla then turned her knees towards mine.

The photographer had been waiting for the precise moment to make it look awkward. He also cropped out the couch and the person Boity was talking to, to make it look like there was tension between the two women. I gave mad props to the photographer for knowing how to find and create a moment, even though he made it seem like it was something it wasn't.

Everybody knows Zodwa Wabantu

In December 2017, I went to New York on a work trip and extended my stay by a few more days. One night, I went to a club with a friend of mine, Selebogo, who is South African and lives between South Africa and New York. He had introduced me to a guy called Troy, who could get me into any club in New York. If we wanted to go to a particular club, we would call him and he would get us access easily.

That night, he'd helped us get into a club that was notoriously difficult to get into, and it was turning out to be a great night.

There was a gentleman manning the restroom. He wore an elegant black waistcoat and a bow tie, with his sleeves rolled up. He had a pleasant and optimistic demeanour about him. I could clearly see that this was just a pit stop for him and not too long from now, he would not only be singing, 'Started from the bottom, now we're here' – he would be the embodiment of it. After washing my hands, he offered me a towel to dry them. I detected an accent.

'Hey, man. Where are you from? I'm from South Africa,' I said.

'For real? I'm from Senegal,' he said.

'No way! You know, I have never been,' I said.

He told me it had been three years since he had been back but he had been in the States for 10 years. He said he had heard that South Africa is beautiful and well developed, and that he would love to go some time if it were not for the xenophobia. I did not want to defend xenophobic actions, of course, but I also wanted to provide perspective. I told him that, on a day-to-day basis, it is not as bad as it has been reported in the news, but it can be bad when you are affected.

While we were chatting, one of the huge bouncers I had met outside came in to relieve himself. 'He is also from Senegal,' said the gentleman I'd been chatting to, as he gestured to the bouncer and introduced me as being from South Africa. The bouncer gave me a smile, suddenly becoming a very different person to the one standing at the door and paid to intimidate. He shook my hand with a great deal of enthusiasm.

'It's great to see a brother from the continent. We don't see a lot of our people coming to this club.' We continued chatting for some time and then he began to tell me about how beautiful South African women are. He didn't think there was a country that had women who rivalled them.

Then, out of nowhere, his face lit up and he whipped out his phone from his pocket. He started clicking and scrolling.

'Do you know this girl?' he asked as he continued to scroll with his massive thumb, which was probably as big as my wrist.

'Which girl?' I asked.

Eventually he put the phone in my hand. He paced up and down, putting his massive hands behind his head and shaking it in disbelief. The expression on his face was that of man who could not comprehend the beauty he was showing me.

I looked down.

'Yes, I know her. Well, not personally, but I know of her,' I said, 'Everybody knows Zodwa Wabantu in South Africa.'

'Oh, my God! What a woman! You South Africans are lucky.'

I was flummoxed. Zodwa Wabantu is known all the way in New York, by a bouncer I just happened to talk to? I began to wonder how big of a phenomenon she might actually be, and we don't even know.

In defence of small talk

I've decided to defend small talk. Let me know if you agree or not.
One of the things that confuses me about us modern Africans is our sudden hatred for small talk. The idea of 'small talk' is actually foreign, maybe even a Western concept. It became fashionable to say that we hate small talk once we started hearing that there was such a thing.

I don't know when I first heard that there was such a thing as small talk. But what I am sure of is that it was not something I ever heard people complaining about in the villages or townships.

In the village, people talk simply for the enjoyment of engaging in conversation, not because there is some deep philosophical discussion taking place. It's just people enjoying each other. Rarely will two strangers simply walk past each other. They will exchange pleasantries before carrying on. Time is not more important than people.

In fact, the pleasantries will carry on, even after they have said goodbye and are walking in opposite directions. People will keep talking to each other until their voices fade. This is the beauty that we are losing.

As Steve Biko put it, 'Westerners have on so many occasions been surprised at the capacity we have for talking to one another

Small talk between my aunt and mother

– not for the sake of arriving at a particular conclusion but merely to enjoy the communication for its own sake.' And he went on to say that, 'No one felt unnecessarily an intruder into someone else's business.' Perhaps we call it small talk now because we have lost the art of ukuncokola (conversation for its own sake). Or we are just too busy hurrying off to places and things.

An American being an American in America

The year they called Coachella 'Beychella' my friends and I decided to go under the guise of celebrating my birthday when it really was because everyone wanted to go watch Beyoncé. It was myself, Thoba Mkangisa, Troy Gordon and of course, Xolisa Dyeshana, as well as Unathi Mdoda, Anele Mdoda, Zamalisa Mdoda …Yes, it was almost the whole Mdoda clan. Unfortunately, Thembisa Mdoda couldn't make it because work just wouldn't let her be great. Sizwe Dhlomo also couldn't make it because he had a test to write. I don't know if Anele, Beyoncé's biggest fan, will ever forgive Sizwe for missing out over a mere test.

At Coachella, we would mostly wake up at leisure then head over to have breakfast at the resort. None of us were in any hurry. We aimed to relax and enjoy the moments as much as we could. The only thing that would spark any real heat (other than the 39-degree Celsius temperatures) was someone trying to debate whether Beyoncé had surpassed Michael Jackson or not. Otherwise, everyone was consistently calm.

One morning, after a long breakfast, which had lasted a solid two hours, Xolisa and I decided to go sit outside on some comfortable garden furniture under a big tree. The couches were half-moon shaped and each half-moon could sit four people with a small round table in the middle for drinks.

I went to the restroom (I still don't know why it is called that because there is no reason to want to rest there. Why would any-one want to rest with their urine – or worse, their number two?) and when I returned, I found Xolisa speaking to a white lady in her sixties.

'You're from South Africa too?' she asked as I perched my slightly larger-than-average ass on the couch. I was wearing shorts that showed off my ridiculously sexy legs.

'Yes,' I replied to the o' lady. She wore a straw hat to protect herself from the hell-hot, blazing sun of Coachella Valley.

'You also came here for the festival?' she asked me. She seemed to be the most unassuming person in the universe, but it was not long before I figured out that she was insanely wealthy – just by how she spoke.

'Yes, I did,' I said, and began to launch into a monologue about how amazing the previous day was. She put her hand on her cheek. She was clearly unsure.

Her son then joined her and she introduced us.

She turned to him. 'Can you believe it? They came all the way here from South Africa – just for a music festival,' she said disapprovingly. The son was just as incredulous.

'Can you believe that some people fly all the way from America to South Africa, just to see lions and elephants?' I retorted.

The challenges black professionals face in the workplace

A few years ago, when I had resigned from a large and reputable company, five of the directors each called me to their offices to ask why I was leaving. I had such a great future in the company, they said.

Eventually, I had a meeting with the president of the company, who also wanted to know why I'd chosen to move on. I explained to her that I had a lot that I still wanted to learn and I didn't feel I'd have these opportunities there. I wanted to be scared again. I craved 'not knowing'. She told me she understood, and then she asked me a very important question: 'Why are so many talented young people leaving the company?' I knew that she was really asking why the young black people were leaving.

I didn't claim to be speaking on behalf of anyone, but I told her I would touch on my observations. I felt that people were concerned that they are not being considered for promotions or overseas assignments.

She countered, saying that if she looked at her own career, for example, she had not waited for promotions; she had actively sought people in the organisation to be her champions. She would look for coaches who knew what roles she wanted so that when those opened up, they would think about her first. People are in charge of their own careers, she said.

I agreed wholeheartedly. However, I said, there is lack of consideration for the African cultural context. I gave an example: when schools opened for black children in the early 1990s, the teachers thought I was insubordinate if I didn't look them in the eye – but in the black-only schools I had been to before, I was insubordinate for looking teachers in the eye. That is a cultural nuance.

I also pointed out that there is often a generation gap between directors and the young talent. Culturally, especially where I come from as a black person, it is not acceptable to initiate conversations and to become familiar with older people. You must treat older people with respect and be differential towards them. To approach older professionals for help in a corporate environment means going against something that is innate and becoming familiar with older people. That's already a difficult one.

And over and above that, there is the racial difference and the context of South Africa's history. The senior person who could help you in your career is not often just older but also white. Given the history of this country, we can't dismiss these issues.

I said to the company president that it may be difficult to explain why she likes Mandy from Bryanston more than Lebo from Soweto. But with Mandy, it may be easier to relate to her because they have similar interests and more things in common than with Lebo. Therefore, it stands to reason that an unconscious cultural bias may cause her to be more connected with Mandy and may cause her to think about Mandy first when a promotion comes up.

I recommended that the company implement a system for directors to actively seek out mentees and to break down those cultural gaps, by understanding that they exist and not expecting everyone to be like Mandy.

Talent will stay if companies really question why people are leaving rather than complaining about it. I was fortunate to be able to connect with many directors in the company and give them my views. But the system is rigged against blackness and the powers that be in corporates are often blind to it and don't want to be told about these uncomfortable realities.

It is also a false notion that black talent feels entitled to seniority at a fast pace. I don't believe this is true. Those who are great at what they do know that it takes time to hone their skills and be at the top of their game. They don't expect to get into a company today and be chief executive tomorrow. They just want a fair chance to realise their ambitions.

But how do you get a fair chance where nothing is really fair?

What many people fail to grasp is the reason for affirmative action legislation in the first place: some companies have had to be forced to look for, find and hire black talent. In the past, these companies simply refused and said there were no qualified black people. Yet many new employees learn on the job and become qualified while doing it.

There is also the false idea that affirmative action means kicking people out of jobs. The way I see it, it means creating an expanding economy. Giving a black person a job does not mean getting rid of a white person.

In another chapter, I've spoken about how being in a privileged position, with access to financial, educational and networking opportunities, can greatly influence a person's success in life. The reality of South Africa's history is that black people have not had access to these opportunities, but instead, have often had to work twice as hard as their white counterparts simply to be given half the chances. Someone who does not experience this, who does not live it, will view affirmative action as black entitlement, rather than an attempt to set things right.

I have been hearing some disturbing accounts about what is happening to deserving black talent in some industries.

One such story involved a black person working for a reputable firm in the financial sector. A senior individual was vacating a position and for two years, it was a given in the organisation that this black female would logically fill the post – she had been with the firm for some time and had been performing some of the tasks already. When the time came, even after she'd been preparing for the position for two years, she was passed over and the job was given to someone who was her junior – and white. A staff member in the HR department questioned this decision but the HR head simply explained that the order to pass over the black woman for a junior white person came from above and there was nothing he could do.

Now, this is the dilemma black people often face.

As I've explained in another chapter, as a black person, your abilities at work are often doubted simply because you are black. In many work environments, you have to prove over and over again that you are good enough. Your mistakes are scrutinised more. While you are seen to have potential, your white colleague is regarded as someone who is already ready for the next step.

I recently heard of one case where the directors of a financial institution were talking about how they had produced the highest number of qualified black people. An intern asked, 'How come there isn't a single black person in senior management then?' He was told that his question was ridiculous. When his internship ended, he did not get paid.

These questions are not ridiculous. They are important, and the answers – even when they are complex – are just as important. These conversations may be uncomfortable – for the black professionals who fear stagnation or victimisation at work for rocking the boat, and for some white employers who would rather not hear about these black-and-white issues – but we need to have them because if we don't, the changes we all need to make will take an even longer time.

What I have learnt

I have learnt:

1. It's never as easy as people think it is.
2. Just because it looks like someone had it easy doesn't mean they did.
3. People will criticise you for doing well, and will mock you for doing right. Keep doing it anyway.
4. It's easier for us to remember the negative things people say about us than the positive words others say to us. Be deliberate about remembering the positive.
5. You can't make everyone like you. Not everyone will, nor should they. When you try to please everyone, you end up not being pleased with yourself.
6. You don't have all the answers.
7. The most important thing is to be honest with yourself. If you can't be truthful to yourself, you will be hurt easily by what others say about you.
8. When you love yourself, it's hard to hate.
9. No one criticises your efforts more than an underachiever.
10. Finding your purpose is a lifelong journey.

11. Very few people know what they were born to do. Most of us have to keep discovering the reason for our being, little by little.
12. Life is full of delicious surprises.
13. Never settle for a comfortable existence.
14. It is okay not to know.

Acknowledgements

As in *To Quote Myself*, the first person I want to thank is my mother who, after being sent the cover of this book via WhatsApp, responded with: 'Khona kutheni uthi ithandwa ngumamakho? Uyifunde phi umama waselalini, xa ndifuna uku-hambahamba elalini ukufumana umntu, ngubani oza kundifundela andicacisele yona?' ('Why do you say your mom liked it? Where would a simple village woman have read it, when I need to walk around the village to find someone who will read it and explain it to me?') She has been instrumental in reminding me about parts of my childhood, and has a sharp sense of humour that always brings me down to earth.

Thank you to my sister, Sikelelwa Dlanga, who continues to be a positive force in my life. She has also helped me to remember many stories; even though some of these may not have made it into this book, they inspired me to write about other memories.

I asked Donovan Goliath to work on a cover image for this book because I love the clever, conceptual designs he posts on Instagram (@donovangoliath). I fell in love with the idea he shared with me as soon as he told me about it. Thank you, Donovan. Let's enter this cover for some awards.

I would also like to thank Trevor Noah for taking the time to read through my book and then offering his opinion for us to use on the front cover.

About a month before my publisher asked me for my most dashing photograph, Saki Zamxaka had called a few of us over to have fun with his camera in his home studio. One of the pictures he took ended up being used for the cover of this book. Thank you, Saki, for always brandishing your camera.

And thanks to the publishing team who has worked with me on all my books: Andrea Nattrass at Pan Macmillan with her ever-present whip and threats; Kelly Norwood-Young, my patient editor who really gets my voice (I insisted on her again for this book; incidentally, she was pregnant with her first child when she edited *To Quote Myself* and her second baby is due shortly after we publish this one – between babies and my books, she has four children!); Sean Fraser, the meticulous proofreader; and Kevin Shenton, the layout wizard.

There are also many people who have been involved in my stories. Some of these people are close to me; some I've only met once and will never meet again. Whether for a brief moment or a lifetime, they've all been co-stars in my life and they've all had an impact. Thank you to every person who has made these stories possible, because through you, I find the joy that is in my life.